THE USBORNE
INTERNET-LINKED
INTRODUCTION TO
ASIA

ISBN 0-439-88982-0
Copyright © 2005 by Usborne Publishing Ltd. All rights reserved. Published by Scholastic Inc., 557 Broadway, New York, NY 10012, by arrangement with Usborne Publishing Ltd. The name Usborne and the devices ⊕ ♀ are trademarks of Usborne Publishing Ltd. SCHOLASTIC and associated logos are trademarks and/or registered trademarks of Scholastic Inc.

12 11 10 9 8 7 6 5 4 3 2 1   6 7 8 9 10 11/0
Printed in the U.S.A.   40
First Scholastic printing, November 2006

Cover: A man rides a decorated elephant, in the city of Jaipur in northern India
Previous page: The Buddhist temple complex at Borobudur, on the Indonesian island of Java
This page: Night fishermen on the Li River in China, near Guilin

THE USBORNE
INTERNET-LINKED
INTRODUCTION TO
ASIA

Elizabeth Dalby

SCHOLASTIC INC.

New York Toronto London Auckland Sydney
Mexico City New Delhi Hong Kong Buenos Aires

Designed by Joanne Kirkby, Karen Tomlins,
Candice Whatmore and Kate Rimmer

Digital imagery by Keith Furnival and Joanne Kirkby

Edited by Kirsteen Rogers

Consultants: Professor Michael Hitchcock, London Metropolitan University
and Professor Ulrich Kratz, School of Oriental and African Studies

Cartography: European Map Graphics Ltd

Consultant cartographic editor: Craig Asquith

Internet links

Throughout this book, we have suggested interesting websites where you can find out more about Asia. To visit the sites, go to the Usborne Quicklinks Website at **www.usborne-quicklinks.com** and type the keyword "asia". There you will find links to click on to take you to all the sites. Here are some of the things you can do on the websites:

- Take a snapshot tour of India's incredible landscapes and wildlife.

- Follow the tea trail to find out how tea is produced, and then try a tea-related crossword, quiz and wordsearch.

- Explore the Kamchatka Peninsula and meet some of the creatures that live there.

INTERNET LINK

For a link to a website with an introduction to Japanese calligraphy, and a chance to try virtual calligraphy, go to **www.usborne-quicklinks.com**

Internet safety

When using the Internet, please follow these guidelines:

- Ask your parent's or guardian's permission before you connect to the Internet.

- If you write a message in a website guest book or on a website message board, do not include any personal information such as your full name, address or telephone number, and ask an adult before you give your email address.

- If a website asks you to log in or register by typing your name or email address, ask permission of an adult first.

- If you do receive an email from someone you don't know, tell an adult and do not reply to the email.

- Never arrange to meet anyone you have talked to on the Internet.

Site availability

The links in Usborne Quicklinks are regularly reviewed and updated, but occasionally you may get a message that a site is unavailable. This might be temporary, so try again later, or even the next day. If any of the sites close down, we will, if possible, replace them with suitable alternatives, so you will always find an up-to-date list of sites in Usborne Quicklinks.

Look for descriptions of recommended websites on the pages of this book, then go to the Usborne Quicklinks Website for links to all the sites.

Note for parents and guardians

The websites described in this book are regularly reviewed and the links in Usborne Quicklinks are updated. However, the content of a website may change at any time and Usborne Publishing is not responsible for the content on any website other than its own.

We recommend that children are supervised while on the Internet, that they do not use Internet chat rooms, and that you use Internet filtering software to block unsuitable material. Please ensure that your children read and follow the safety guidelines printed on the left. For more information, see the "Net Help" area on the Usborne Quicklinks Website.

Computer not essential

If you don't have access to the Internet, don't worry. This book is a complete, self-contained reference book on its own.

Contents

Lanterns for the Chinese New Year festival hang outside a shop in Vietnam. They symbolize long life and good luck.

Two Indian women lay newly dyed cotton fabric out to dry in the hot sun, in the desert region of Rajasthan.

Introduction to Asia

Asia is by far the biggest continent in the world. It contains every kind of landscape, from ice and snow to scorched, arid deserts, and from windswept grasslands to lush, tropical rainforests, as well as many of the Earth's highest mountain ranges. Asia is made up of around 50 countries, including some of the world's largest and most densely populated. Over half of all the people on Earth live in Asia, and their religions, cultures, languages and traditions have a huge influence across the world.

In this book, the continent of Asia has been divided into regions, shown on the map over the page. Each section begins with an introduction to the region and a map of the countries in it. Read on to find out about the area's landscapes, climate, crops and wildlife, as well as its natural resources and environmental issues. You can also take a look at the people who live there – their towns and cities, their religions, art, culture, entertainment and everyday life.

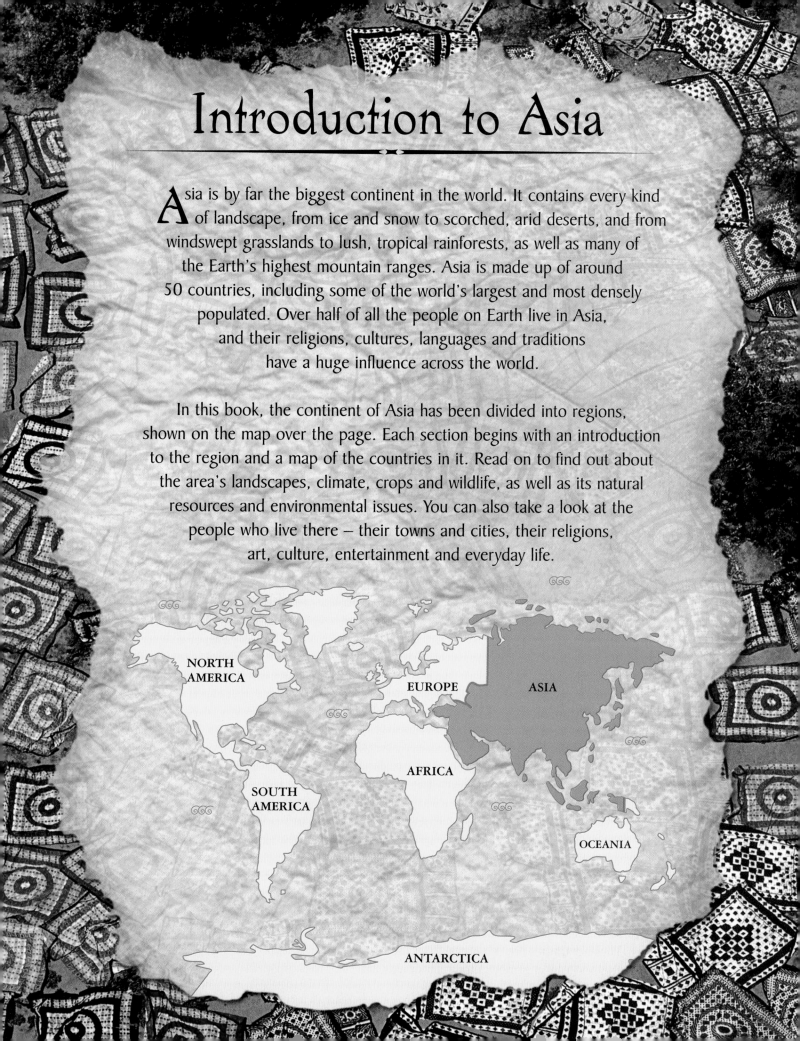

NORTH AMERICA

EUROPE

ASIA

AFRICA

SOUTH AMERICA

OCEANIA

ANTARCTICA

Map of Asia

All the countries that make up Asia are shown on this map, as well as capital cities and the names of seas and oceans. The map has been shaded to show the different regions that are featured in this book.

Key to map of Asia

- ■ Capital city
- ----- Boundary between Asia and Europe
- ▬▬ Borders between countries
- —— Coastlines
- ▓ Lakes and inland seas
- 🌀🌀🌀 Seas
- 〰 Rivers

0km   1,000km
0 miles   640 miles

Central Asia

Central Asia includes Kazakhstan, Turkmenistan, Uzbekistan, Kyrgyzstan, Tajikistan, Afghanistan and Mongolia. Mongolia is a little way to the east of the other countries in the region, but the people living there share a similar way of life with the people in the other Central Asian countries.

The Indian Subcontinent

The Indian Subcontinent includes India, Pakistan, Nepal, Bhutan, Bangladesh, Sri Lanka and the Maldives. These countries are separated from the rest of Asia to the north by enormous mountain ranges.

ARCTIC OCEAN

Franz Josef Land

Severnaya Zemlya

Novaya Zemlya

Barents Sea

Kara Sea

Yenisey

Moscow

RUSSIA

Ob

Volga

EUROPE / ASIA

Black Sea

Ankara

TURKEY

GEORGIA

ARMENIA

AZERBAIJAN

Astana

KAZAKHSTAN

Aral Sea

CYPRUS

LEBANON
Beirut

SYRIA
Damascus

Jerusalem
ISRAEL
Amman

JORDAN

Baghdad

IRAQ

Caspian Sea

Tehran

UZBEKISTAN

TURKMENISTAN

Ashgabat

Tashkent

Bishkek

KYRGYZSTAN

Dushanbe

TAJIKISTAN

IRAN

AFGHANISTAN

Kabul

Islamabad

Indus

SAUDI ARABIA

KUWAIT

Riyadh

BAHRAIN

Doha
QATAR

Abu Dhabi

UNITED ARAB EMIRATES

Muscat

PAKISTAN

New Delhi

NEPAL
Kathmandu

BHUTAN
Thimphu

Dhaka

BANGLADESH

Ganges

INDIA

Sana

OMAN

YEMEN

Arabian Sea

Bay of Bengal

Socotra (Yemen)

INDIAN OCEAN

Andaman Islands (India)

SRI LANKA
Sri Jayewardenepura Kotte

Colombo

Nicobar Islands (India)

MALDIVES
Male

There are more detailed, regional maps of Asia on pages 74–85, showing many more towns and cities as well as mountains, rivers and other types of landscapes.

Russia

Russia is the largest country in Asia and although a small part of it is actually in Europe, the whole country is included in this book. Moscow, Russia's capital, is in the European part, and things that happen there often affect the country as a whole. As it is part of both continents, Russia considers itself both Asian and European.

Eastern Asia

Eastern Asia includes China, Japan, North Korea, South Korea and Taiwan. Japan, Taiwan and North and South Korea have all been influenced by China's culture and way of life.

Mainland Southeast Asia

Mainland Southeast Asia includes Laos, Burma (Myanmar), Vietnam, Thailand and Cambodia. These countries share similar cultures and languages, and the Buddhist faith is an important part of everyday life.

Maritime Southeast Asia

Maritime Southeast Asia includes Malaysia, Indonesia, the Philippines, Singapore, East Timor and Brunei. These countries form a vast group of islands that spread across the South China Sea, to the south and east of mainland Asia.

The Middle East

The countries shown in white make up the region known as the Middle East and are not covered in this book.

9

Russian soldiers stand in Red Square in Moscow, Russia's capital city. The silhouetted building in the background is St. Basil's Cathedral, which has distinctive, onion-shaped domes.

Russia

Russia is by far the biggest country in the world and it takes seven days to cross it by train. The smaller part of Russia to the west of the Ural Mountains is in Europe, but the much larger, eastern part stretches across all of northern Asia. Eastern Russia is often called Siberia.

Siberia is notoriously cold. Almost all of Russia's northern coast is inside the Arctic Circle, and most of the land farther south is covered in freezing forest. Where southern Russia meets the countries of Central Asia, the forest gives way to rolling, windswept grasslands and fields of wheat and cotton.

Siberian snowscapes

Freezing forests

Much of northern Russia is covered in *taiga* forest. The word *taiga* comes from Russian and is used to describe cold, evergreen forests. Russia's *taiga* is the largest forested area in the world – twice as big as the Amazon rainforest in South America. Despite the freezing climate, many animals live in the *taiga*, including brown bears, snow leopards and Siberian tigers. But the *taiga* is shrinking, as trees are cut down for timber. Even if trees are replanted, the climate is so cold that the new trees take many years to grow.

This snowy pine forest is in Yakutia, in the far northeastern corner of Russia, near the Verkhoyansk mountains. Very few people live in this isolated area.

A group of Russian boys has cleared a patch of snow away from the frozen surface of Lake Baikal, for a game of ice hockey.

Lake Baikal

The deepest lake on Earth is Lake Baikal, in southern Siberia. If the lake were emptied, it would take 400 years for the rivers that flow into it to fill it again. The huge amount of water in Lake Baikal affects the climate near its shores, because water heats up and cools down much more slowly than land does. Near the lake, the summers are cooler and the winters are milder than they are in the rest of Siberia. Even so, in winter, the lake freezes over with a layer of ice thick enough to skate on or even drive across.

INTERNET LINK

For a link to a website where you can find out about the volcanic wilderness of the Kamchatka Peninsula in eastern Russia, go to **www.usborne-quicklinks.com**

The Arctic north

The extreme northern fringe of Russia's land, deep inside the Arctic Circle, is tundra – a flat, marshy, treeless plain, lashed by biting winds. The ground there contains a thick layer called permafrost that stays frozen solid all year round. This prevents large plants and trees from taking root.

Creatures that live on the tundra include many species of tiny flies and mosquitoes. There are also small mammals, such as ground squirrels and lemmings, and much larger mammals like caribou and musk oxen. These large tundra animals are always on the move, trying to find new pastures that they can raid for food.

Arctic ground squirrels live on the Siberian tundra, where they search for grasses, mushrooms and berries to eat.

Kamchatka Peninsula

The Kamchatka Peninsula sticks out from Russia like a tongue, into the Pacific Ocean. It's an area of stunning natural wilderness with many active, rumbling volcanoes, bubbling hot springs and erupting jets of hot water called geysers. The mountains are carved into jagged shapes by slowly flowing rivers of ice called glaciers. This region is one of the most active parts of a huge, arc-shaped zone of volcanoes that surrounds the Pacific Ocean.

This rocky crater, on one of the volcanoes on the Kamchatka Peninsula, is partly filled by a brilliant blue-green lake, which is heated by volcanic activity from below.

Beliefs and lifestyles

Orthodox Christianity

Many Russians are Orthodox Christians. Orthodox churches are adorned with gold decorations and icons – painted pictures of saints. Peals of bells call people to lavish church ceremonies which include rituals such as burning candles, and are accompanied by passionate singing. During the 20th century, Russia's Communist leaders discouraged all religions, but Orthodox Christianity survived, and today it is becoming more popular once again.

Onion-shaped domes are typical of Russian Orthodox churches like this, the Church of the Transfiguration on Kizhi Island, near Moscow. The domes were originally designed to allow snow to fall off easily in Russia's cold climate.

Links with Mongolia

A part of Siberia, south of Lake Baikal, is home to many Buryat people. It was once part of the vast Mongolian empire, which stretched from central Asia to China. Many people there share beliefs with people living in present-day Mongolia, such as Buddhism and shamanism (spirit worship), and they also wear similar traditional costumes.

These Siberian girls are wearing traditional summer costumes, similar to those worn by people living in Mongolia and parts of China.

This man belongs to a group of people called the Nenets, who live in Siberia. He is leading a caravan of reindeer, and is warmly dressed in a coat made of reindeer fur.

Reindeer herders

In Russia's far north live the Nenets people. They are reindeer herders who travel across the tundra with their herds, between summer and winter pastures. Reindeer provide the Nenets with milk and meat, as well as fur and skins for clothing and shelter against the freezing environment. The Nenets are constantly on the move, searching for spongy plants called lichen that the reindeer can eat. They sleep in tents made of branches covered in reindeer skins.

INTERNET LINK

To take an interactive journey with the Nenets people and find out more about their way of life, go to **www.usborne-quicklinks.com**

Russian delicacies

Some foods in Russia have special significance. In everyday life, no meal is complete without bread, and when important people visit, they may be greeted with a gift of bread and salt. Certain festivals have foods associated with them, such as the Easter cheesecake called *pashka*. But one of Russia's most famous foods, and also one of the world's most expensive, is caviar. This delicacy is made from the eggs of sturgeon fish, which live mainly in the Caspian Sea.

Caviar from the Caspian Sea is sold in tiny tins like these. The cost of a single tin could feed a whole Russian family for up to a week.

Arts and crafts

Brave writers

Russian folk tales such as the *Firebird* and the *Snowmaiden* have been told for hundreds of years, to generations of children. But Russia's written literature first became famous worldwide in the 19th century, when writers published novels, plays and poetry to express their discontent with their country's politics. Some Russian writers got into trouble for their views, and suffered terrible punishments, such as exile to Siberia and death sentences.

Anton Chekhov wrote plays about Russian life around the start of the 20th century. One of his most famous is *The Seagull*.

World-famous ballet

Ballet came to Russia in the 18th century from France, and became a great art form there in the 19th and early 20th centuries. Choreographers worked with composers such as Tchaikovsky and Stravinsky to produce spectacular and ground-breaking performances. Two Russian ballet companies are now world-famous – the Kirov of St. Petersburg and the Bolshoi of Moscow. Young ballet dancers train hard from an early age in the hope of one day performing with them.

These Russian dolls fit inside each other. They are painted to look like girls dressed in peasant-style clothes.

Traditional crafts

Because Russia has huge areas of forest, many of its traditional crafts make use of wood. Some examples include painted religious icons and exquisitely carved toys. Lacquered wooden Easter eggs are traditional in Russia, and from this style developed dolls called *Matryoshka* – sets of hollow, differently sized wooden dolls that fit perfectly inside one another.

INTERNET LINK
For a link to a website where you can
read the story behind the *Nutcracker* ballet,
go to **www.usborne-quicklinks.com**

Chess in Russia

Vladimir Lenin, a former Russian leader, was an avid chess player. He encouraged all Russians to play this ancient Asian game, believing that it helped disciplined thought. Chess in Russia had traditionally been a game played only by the wealthy, but it quickly became widely popular. Schools were set up for excellent young players, and Russia has ever since been known for its high standard of chess.

Russian girls play chess at their school
near Lake Baikal in southern Siberia.

In 2001, the Moscow Ballet performed a new version of the *Nutcracker*, featuring the Dove of Peace. This was to celebrate lasting peace between Russia and the USA, who were once enemies.

In Mongolia, men use golden eagles to help them hunt. Eagles are trained from a young age to catch prey such as rabbits, foxes, deer and wolves, which the hunters use for their skins. After ten years, the eagles are released into the wild, to breed.

Central Asia

*Kazakhstan, Turkmenistan, Uzbekistan, Tajikistan,
Kyrgyzstan, Afghanistan, Mongolia*

The dusty, windswept countries of Central Asia are bordered in
the south and east by high, bleak mountain ranges – the Tien
Shan, the Hindu Kush, the Pamirs and the Karakorum. Large areas of
Kazakhstan and Turkmenistan are covered in open grassland, and
much of Uzbekistan is hot desert, while Tajikistan, Kyrgyzstan and
Afghanistan are crowded with towering, snowy peaks. All these
countries, apart from Afghanistan, were once part of one enormous
country known as the USSR, governed by Russia from Moscow.

Mongolia, to the east, shares similarities with these countries,
although it is not always considered part of Central Asia. It too is
covered in empty grasslands and deserts. Many of its people move
around with their herds as they do in other Central Asian countries.

KAZAKHSTAN

Irtysh

Aral Sea

Caspian Sea

Lake Balkhash

MONGOLIA

Altai Mountains

UZBEKISTAN

TURKMENISTAN

Kara Kum Desert

Gobi Desert

KYRGYZSTAN

Tien Shan

Pamirs

TAJIKISTAN

Hindu Kush

AFGHANISTAN

0km   1,000km
0 miles   640 miles

Peaks and plains

Tajikistan's peaks

The eastern part of Tajikistan is sometimes called the roof of the world because it is completely covered by the towering peaks of the Pamirs, the world's second highest range of mountains. So much of Tajikistan is mountainous that only around one-tenth of its land is suitable for farming.

People can't survive for long on very high mountains, but some do manage to live on the lower mountain slopes. As a result of its scenic rocky landscape, Tajikistan is one of the world's poorest countries.

These mist-swathed peaks are part of the Pamir mountain range, in northern Pakistan, near Tajikistan.

Grasslands of Asia

Much of central Asia is covered in dry grassland called *steppe*. It stretches across Asia, from the eastern edge of Europe to northern China, and is the biggest area of grassland in the world.

There are few trees to give shade or shelter, so it's hot on the *steppe* in summer, but bitterly cold in winter. There's very little rain, and strong winds whip across the flat landscape. Luckily, the grasses have long, intertwined roots to anchor themselves firmly in the ground against the strong gusts. Common grassland animals include rodents such as gerbils, mice and hamsters. There are also herds of grazing animals such as sheep, cattle and camels, belonging to farmers.

Mongolia is home to both wild and tame horses. They graze on its vast grasslands.

INTERNET LINK

For a link to a website where you can take a virtual sightseeing trip in the Pamirs, go to **www.usborne-quicklinks.com**

Jewel of Kyrgyzstan

One of Kyrgyzstan's most stunning natural features is Lake Issyk, a deep, clear lake nestled between ridges of the Tien Shan mountains, which form the country's border with China.

The lake is surrounded by towns and health resorts, as people believe that bathing in the lake's mineral-rich waters is good for them. The water is too salty for humans to drink or to use for watering the land nearby, but cattle are able to drink it. Many kinds of fish live in the lake, and it also provides a winter home for migrating water birds, because it never completely freezes over, even in deepest winter.

The dark patch below is Lake Issyk in Kyrgyzstan, between the high, snowy peaks of the Tien Shan mountain range. This photograph was taken from space by a satellite.

A man on camelback travels across the baked, arid landscape of the Kara Kum Desert in Turkmenistan.

Turkmenistan's desert

Turkmenistan is a spacious country, but few people live there, as it is mostly covered by the sandy wastes of the Kara Kum Desert. Its towns are built close to what little water there is, such as the man-made canal that runs through the desert. The desert is also dotted with places called oases where there's enough water for things to grow. The capital, Ashgabat, is built around an oasis in the south of the country.

As well as being dry, the Kara Kum Desert is also hot. Among the few kinds of animals that can survive such harsh conditions are spiders, scorpions and giant monitor lizards.

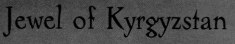

Harsh landscapes

Russian rockets

The Baikonur Cosmodrome in Kazakhstan is the site of many of Russia's rocket launches. These provide money for both countries, as companies pay Russia to send satellites into orbit, and Russia pays Kazakhstan to use the land. There are serious drawbacks – used metal rocket parts rain down on Kazakhstan, and the toxic rocket chemicals affect the health of people living near Baikonur.

This rocket is on its way to the launch pad at the Baikonur Cosmodrome in Kazakhstan.

Cotton is one of the crops grown in Afghanistan to be sold to other countries. These men are weighing cotton for sale at a market.

Cotton-growing countries

Kazakhstan, Uzbekistan, Turkmenistan, Kyrgyzstan and Tajikistan, which were once part of the USSR, contain vast stretches of flat land. The Moscow government used large areas of these countries to grow cotton, to be sold abroad. When they became independent in 1991, the countries were at last free to decide for themselves which crops to grow. Sadly, the years of intensive cotton farming had used up an enormous amount of precious river water and much of the land had become desert, unsuitable for new farms. Today there are still many cotton farms, which provide a useful source of income for the countries.

Aral Sea disaster

The Aral Sea has shrunk to one-third of its original size within the last fifty years, and could dry out completely during this century. This environmental disaster happened because water from the rivers that feed the lake was diverted for watering cotton crops. The Aral Sea's fishing and shipping industries have been ruined, and the air around it is now so dry and salty that it badly affects the health of many people living nearby.

A fishing boat stranded on dry land in Kazakhstan shows where the Aral Sea used to reach, before it began to dry up.

An Afghan family travels on the back of a donkey. Until recently, Afghan women were forced to cover their faces, as this woman has done.

INTERNET LINK

For a link to a website where you can see amazing photographs of fallen rockets and space junk from the Baikonur Cosmodrome, go to **www.usborne-quicklinks.com**

Nomadic herders

Many Central Asian people lead nomadic lives, which means they move regularly between different pastures with their herds of animals. The animals provide meat and milk as well as skins and wool for clothing and shelter. Nomadic people in Central Asia need to move around frequently, as much of the ground there is so dry that their animals quickly eat up all the available food.

Nomads get some of the extra things they need for themselves by trading with people living in the towns that they pass through on their travels. The townspeople need leather and meat, which the nomads supply in return for grain for their animals, cotton and silk thread, as well as metal and pottery objects such as knives and cooking pots.

Traditional life

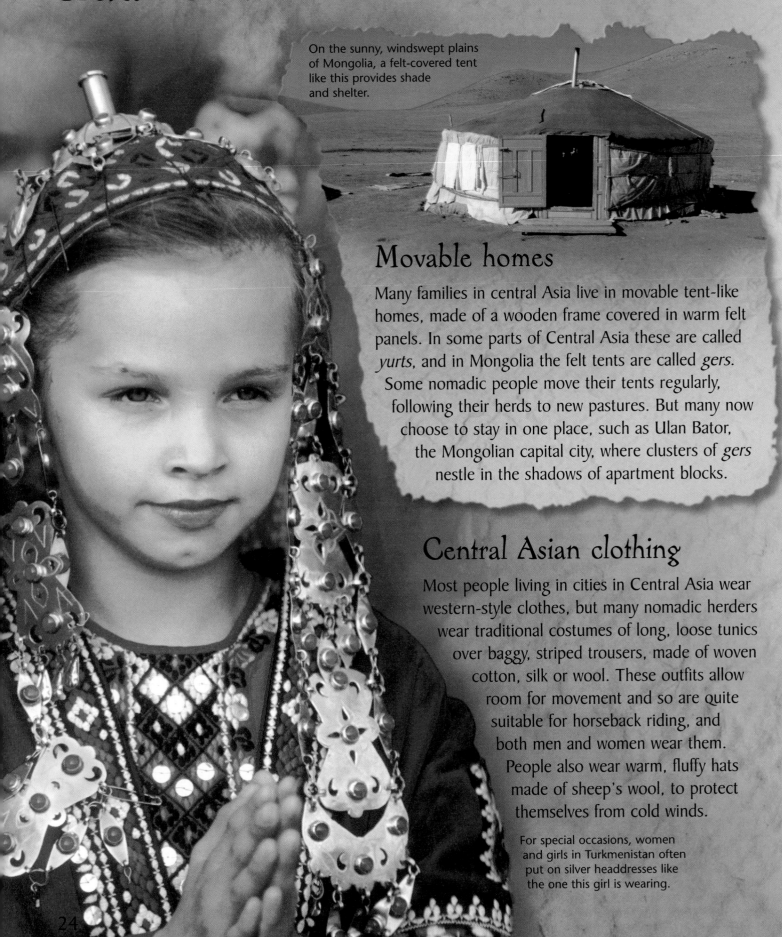

On the sunny, windswept plains of Mongolia, a felt-covered tent like this provides shade and shelter.

Movable homes

Many families in central Asia live in movable tent-like homes, made of a wooden frame covered in warm felt panels. In some parts of Central Asia these are called *yurts*, and in Mongolia the felt tents are called *gers*. Some nomadic people move their tents regularly, following their herds to new pastures. But many now choose to stay in one place, such as Ulan Bator, the Mongolian capital city, where clusters of *gers* nestle in the shadows of apartment blocks.

Central Asian clothing

Most people living in cities in Central Asia wear western-style clothes, but many nomadic herders wear traditional costumes of long, loose tunics over baggy, striped trousers, made of woven cotton, silk or wool. These outfits allow room for movement and so are quite suitable for horseback riding, and both men and women wear them. People also wear warm, fluffy hats made of sheep's wool, to protect themselves from cold winds.

For special occasions, women and girls in Turkmenistan often put on silver headdresses like the one this girl is wearing.

Cities of Uzbekistan

A trade route which became known as the Silk Road once stretched across Asia. As well as silk, many other goods and ideas spread along the route. Buddhism reached China and Japan from India, while gunpowder and porcelain were introduced to Europe from China. The Silk Road passed through Uzbekistan, and its magnificent cities are filled with buildings covered in carvings and mosaics, constructed hundreds of years ago when the Silk Road was busiest.

Mongolian holy men

As in many other Asian countries, most people in Mongolia follow the Buddhist faith. Mongolia has its own particular kind of Buddhism with certain beliefs, ceremonies and features. For example, in Mongolia holy men called *lamas* make a living by providing people with advice about religious, medical or spiritual problems. *Lamas* also bless projects such as new buildings.

INTERNET LINK

For a link to a website where you can see how a *yurt* is built, go to **www.usborne-quicklinks.com**

This dome covered in mosaic tiles tops one of the buildings in the Registan, the main central square of the ancient city of Samarqand, in Uzbekistan.

These boys attend a school where they will learn to be Buddhist holy men, or *lamas*, in Ulan Bator in Mongolia.

www.usborne-quicklinks.com

Riches and finery

Islamic architecture

Most people in Central Asia follow the religion of Islam, and their religious beliefs have influenced the style of architecture there. Buildings are often patterned with paintings and mosaics, but the decorations don't show people or animals, as some followers of Islam believe that humans should not create images of living things. For this reason, designs are made up of geometric shapes and plant-like patterns.

This is a detail from the ceiling of a mosque in Bukhara in Uzbekistan. It is made up of geometric patterns typical of Islamic places of worship.

Amazing carpets

For thousands of years, skilled craftworkers in Turkmenistan have produced exquisite carpets, made from the soft, silky wool of a sheep called the *Saryja*, which is unique to Turkmenistan. The carpets contain millions of individual knots, tied by hand. Carpets are traditionally traded at markets called *bazaars* in large cities and towns, along with camels, sheep and other goods. But these days, it's possible to buy carpets from Turkmenistan over the Internet, too.

Many symbols on carpets like this one from Turkmenistan represent different groups of people.

INTERNET LINK

For a link to a website where you can use your Central Asia knowledge to take part in a Mongolian horse race, go to **www.usborne-quicklinks.com**

Valuable horses

Horses are important in Central Asia to help people travel around, for their meat and for their milk, which can be made into a drink called *koumiss*. *Akhal-Teke* horses, a unique breed from Central Asia and Russia, are lean and light, with incredibly glossy coats. They can survive on very little food and water, but are still able to move extremely fast over long distances.

The sleek *Akhal-Teke* breed of horse is fast and agile. The horse shown here is black, but many *Akhal-Tekes* have shimmering golden coats.

A Mongolian *tsam* dancer's tall, elaborately carved mask has no eye holes, so the dancer inside must look out through the character's mouth.

Mongolian dances

Mongolian *tsam* dances are performed in Buddhist monasteries. The dances are religious rituals intended to pass on messages taken from Buddhist teachings to audiences. As part of their ceremony, *tsam* dances have dramatic songs, dance moves, music from gongs and trumpets as well as the highly decorated costumes of characters. These include animals, people, holy figures and devils, and they all have a range of personalities to help represent various positive and negative influences.

An Indian man rides an Asian elephant that has been hand-painted with decorative patterns for a festival.

The Indian Subcontinent

India, Pakistan, Nepal, Bhutan, Bangladesh, Sri Lanka, Maldives

The area known as the Indian Subcontinent is separated from the rest of Asia by the Himalaya and Hindu Kush mountain ranges. The climates of the countries in this region are affected by winds called monsoons, which give them a wet and a dry season each year.

Everyday life is strongly influenced by religion. Hinduism, Buddhism, Sikhism and Jainism all began in this region and still have many followers, and Islam and Christianity are also popular. There are followers of almost every religion in the world living in these countries today.

0km   1,000km
0 miles   640 miles

Hindu Kush

PAKISTAN

Indus

Himalayas

NEPAL

BHUTAN

Ganges

BANGLADESH

Tropic of Cancer

Arabian Sea

INDIA

Bay of Bengal

Andaman Islands (India)

Nicobar Islands (India)

SRI LANKA

MALDIVES

INDIAN OCEAN

Extreme landscapes

The Ganges

A tiny stream that emerges from a mountain spring on the slopes of the Himalayas eventually becomes a huge river called the Ganges. The Ganges flows across northeastern India and through Bangladesh, where it joins another huge river, the Brahmaputra. The main river then fragments into many smaller channels, forming a river delta that is the largest in the world.

Where the Ganges meets the sea, it passes the Sundarbans, a cluster of islands covered in swampy forests. The varied wildlife there includes the world's last few remaining Royal Bengal tigers.

INTERNET LINK

For a link to a website where you can take a snapshot tour of wildlife on the Indian Subcontinent, and try a Himalayan hiking game, go to **www.usborne-quicklinks.com**

This mysterious-looking photograph, taken from space, shows the River Ganges meeting the sea. The pale blue parts are the river channels of the Ganges flowing into the Indian Ocean, at the top of the picture. The dark blue parts show the land between the river channels.

The monsoon winds bring rain to Bangladesh's farmland every year, making it moist enough to grow crops on.

Monsoon climate

Each year, seasonal winds called monsoons sweep across India and Bangladesh, lashing them with violent rainstorms or bringing dry, scorching weather. When the wind blows from the southwest, it passes over the Indian Ocean and brings heavy rain almost every day. But when the wind blows from the lands in the northeast, it brings no rain, so a dry season follows.

Farmers plant their crops to take advantage of the rainy season. However, if there is not enough rain one year, all the crops may fail. If there is too much rain, there may be devastating floods, and the crops are drowned.

The Thar Desert

Along part of the border between India and Pakistan, the Thar Desert forms a vast expanse of dry sand and gravel. Strong winds shift the dunes, so the rolling landscape is always changing. There is no water in this desert at all, so people who live in the Thar must travel long distances out of the desert, on foot or by camel, to find it.

People in the Thar Desert use camels for travel, either riding them or using them to carry equipment. Camels can survive for days without water, and cope with desert sandstorms by sealing their nostrils shut.

The huge Himalayas

At the northern border of the Indian Subcontinent is the massive Himalaya mountain range. It formed around 55 million years ago, which is quite recent for a range of mountains.

The Earth's surface is made up of large pieces of rock called plates, which move incredibly slowly. This movement is what caused the Himalayas to form. Millions of years ago, India was separate from the Asian continent, but the Indian plate gradually drifted north, until it collided with the Asian plate. The land crumpled into the huge, rocky ridges that we call the Himalayas. The Indian plate is still moving north today, so the Himalayas continue to grow by a tiny amount every year.

A rare, clear view of Mount Everest, on the border between Nepal and China. The mountain is also known by its Tibetan name of Chomolangma, and its Nepalese name, Sagarmatha. It is the highest peak on Earth.

Warm, wet climates

Islands in danger

The Maldives are a group of over 1,000 tiny islands in the Indian Ocean. Many of them have sparkling white sandy beaches and lush groves of palm trees, and are popular travel destinations. The islands formed on coral reefs, made by the rocky skeletons of millions of tiny sea creatures. The Maldives are so low-lying that if the sea level ever rises they could be completely submerged. If the sea were also to become warmer, this could kill the coral, and the creatures and plants that live on it would die.

The green patches you can see are two of the Maldive islands. Coral reefs under the water show as light blue patches.

Each of these Sri Lankan fishermen is perching on a wooden stilt, while he uses a rod to catch fish from the shallow water.

Fishing in Sri Lanka

Sri Lanka is an island off the southern tip of India, surrounded by warm, shallow seas. One of its main industries is fishing. Many Sri Lankan fishermen use traditional methods: some fish from boats made of hollowed-out logs, others from perches on poles called stilts. Each stilt fisherman has his own stilt in a patch of shallow water. They usually fish in the cooler hours at sunrise and sunset, using long rods to catch the fish.

These women are picking tea in Sri Lanka. Each worker picks around twice her weight in tea leaves every day.

Tea plantations

Many hills in India and Sri Lanka are cloaked in bright green tea plants. Tea grows well in warm, moist climates like India's, but it prefers high ground, where mist and clouds protect it from the harshest sunlight. The world's biggest tea-producing region is hilly Assam, in northeast India. The tea plants grow in rows that seem to hug the shapes of the hills, and are kept pruned short to make it easier to pick their leaves. The leaves are dried out, rolled and packaged, to be sold all over the world.

Growing jute

The very wet, warm climate of Bangladesh and northeastern India is ideally suited for growing jute plants. These grow around 3m (10ft) high, and their long stems can be twisted together to make yarn. In the 18th century, jute was used to make ropes for ships. People then found they could weave it and began making it into sacks. These days, jute is used to make anything from woven mats to handbags.

As this man harvests jute plants in Bangladesh, he cuts the stems but leaves the roots behind to rot in the ground.

INTERNET LINK

For a link to a website with interactive, tea-related activities and facts, go to
www.usborne-quicklinks.com

33

Daily life

INTERNET LINK

For a link to a website about the small country of Bhutan, go to **www.usborne-quicklinks.com**

Setting her flower petals afloat on the River Ganges at Varanasi, this woman is making an offering to the Hindu gods.

India's city of pilgrims

All followers of the Hindu faith hope to make at least one religious journey, or pilgrimage, in their lifetime, to the city of Varanasi. During their visit, they bathe in the water of the River Ganges, which they believe to be sacred.

Steps called *ghats* line the riverbanks at Varanasi, leading down to the water's edge. Thousands of people crowd onto the *ghats*, especially at festival times, when they come to float lanterns and petals on the water, or to scatter the ashes of people who have died. Holy men called *sadhus* sit beside the river, ready to perform religious ceremonies for pilgrims visiting the city.

Schools in Pakistan

Most children in Pakistan go to public schools, that are free and open to everyone. But many of these schools are poor and can't provide desks, chairs or books. Private schools have much better facilities, but they're very expensive and few parents can afford them.

The other alternative is a religious school. Funded by religious groups, they are free to students, but open only to boys. Students study the *Qur'an*, the holy book of Islam, with other subjects such as mathematics and languages.

Like many public schools in Pakistan, this village school is very overcrowded. These children are studying in a classroom outside the walls of their school.

34

Bhutanese traditions

Bhutan is a tiny country in the Himalayas with a way of life quite untouched by modern ideas and technology. The capital city, Thimphu, is the only capital in the world with no traffic lights. Where busy roads meet, police direct the traffic from a hexagonal hut in the middle of the road. Thimphu is slowly expanding but new buildings are still built in traditional ways, from rocks, mud, bamboo and wood, decorated with painted patterns of flowers, animals and religious motifs.

Inside this traditional building in Bhutan is a prayer wheel, containing written prayers. Followers of the Buddhist faith believe that spinning the wheel sends prayers out into the world.

Indian cooking

Curries are popular all over India, but there are different kinds and they vary depending on where they come from. Northern Indian curries are made with meat, fish or vegetables cooked with combinations of ground spices such as turmeric, cumin and coriander. They are usually served with flat bread. In southern India, most people tend to be vegetarian. Their curries are seasoned with fiery hot chilies, and usually served with rice.

These bright piles of powders are spices for sale at a market in northern India. They are to be used in cooking.

Place of many religions

Home of Hinduism

There are followers of many faiths in India, but the most popular religion there is Hinduism. Nearby Nepal also has a large Hindu following. Hinduism began in India over 4,000 years ago, making it one of the world's oldest religions. It is still thriving today, with millions of followers, and hundreds of festivals that happen throughout the Hindu year.

A Hindu holy man, or *sadhu*, wears this yellow mark, called a *tilak*, on his head to show that he is a member of a religious group.

Muslim memorial

The Taj Mahal, in India, is one of the world's most well-known Islamic buildings. Its walls and floors are inlaid with countless pieces of semi-precious stones and decorated with verses from the *Qur'an*. It was built by Emperor Shah Jahan in 1631, in memory of his wife, and took more than 20,000 men 22 years to build.

The Taj Mahal is made of white marble, and is reflected in a long pool. Its appearance is transformed throughout the day as light falls on it from different angles.

INTERNET LINK

For a link to a website with information on ancient India, its geography and religions, with stories to read and challenges to complete, go to
www.usborne-quicklinks.com

The origin of Sikhism

Sikhism was founded in the Punjab, a part of Pakistan and India where most people were once either Hindus or Muslims. Sikhism teaches that the truth of religion is the same, whatever a person's chosen faith, and that God sees everyone as equals. Today, Sikhs from all over the world make pilgrimages to the Golden Temple, in Amritsar in India. The temple is in the middle of a lake, which the city is named after: Amritsar means "pool of nectar".

Inside the Golden Temple in Amritsar, a priest reads from the *Adi Granth*, the Sikh holy scriptures.

Buddhist beginnings

Buddhism began near the border between present-day India and Nepal, over 2,500 years ago. Today, Buddhism is still popular in India and Nepal, but it has also spread to many other places in Asia, including China, Japan, Mongolia and many countries in Southeast Asia. Each region has its own style of Buddhism as well as different kinds of religious shrines and temples.

The flags tied to the top of this Buddhist shrine in Nepal have prayers written on them. Buddhists believe that when they flutter in the wind, the prayers are sent out around the world.

Poverty and progress

Indian independence

The countries we know today as India, Bangladesh and Pakistan were once ruled by the British. But the Indian people wanted independence, so during the early 20th century, Mahatma Gandhi led them in a peaceful resistance against British rule.

In 1947, the British granted India independence. The land was divided into Hindu-dominated India and a homeland for Muslims called Pakistan. Many people died in riots as millions of Hindus and Muslims crossed the borders between them. In 1971, East Pakistan became a separate Muslim country called Bangladesh.

Mahatma Gandhi led India's struggle for independence. He dressed in a simple loincloth and shawl to identify with India's poorest people.

The small country of Bangladesh is overpopulated and most of its people are extremely poor. These children live in crowded slums in Dhaka, the capital city.

Bangladesh in poverty

Bangladesh is one of the world's most crowded countries, and one of the poorest. Most people there work for a tiny wage and own no land. If the harvest is bad one year and people need to buy extra food for their families, they can borrow money from their rich, land-owning employers. But this means they are bound to keep working for their employers to pay off their debts.

INTERNET LINK

To find out more about the people and culture of India and Bangladesh, go to **www.usborne-quicklinks.com**

This man is painting a billboard in Mumbai, for *Devdas*, the most expensive and successful Indian movie of all time.

Movies from India

India produces more movies every year than any other country. Many of these are made in the studios of Mumbai, nicknamed "Bollywood" (after its old name of Bombay). Bollywood movies are usually busy and loud, with song and dance routines to tell the story, which is often romantic or dramatic.

Modern India

After India gained independence in 1947, Jawaharlal Nehru, the new prime minister, began to modernize his country. He organized the building of new factories, as well as a system of roads and railways to connect them. Partly as a result of Nehru's reforms, in only a few decades, India has become a world leader in science and technology. Many millions of people in India work in the IT industry, or as scientists helping to develop new products such as medicines.

39

The Great Wall of China winds all the way across northern China. The wall was built gradually, starting over 2,000 years ago, to protect China from invaders from the north.

Eastern Asia

China, Japan, North Korea, South Korea, Taiwan

The biggest country in Eastern Asia is China, and more people
live there than in any other country in the world. China's far
north is covered in low deserts and grasslands, but in the west, a vast area
of highlands forms the Plateau of Tibet, which is overshadowed only by the
Himalayas, the highest mountains in the world. In eastern China there are
large areas of farmland watered by wide rivers, and just off the coast is the
rugged, beautiful island of Taiwan. Above Taiwan, the steep, forest-clad
mountains of the Korean Peninsula jut out into the East China Sea. To the
far east, the country of Japan is made up of a long chain of volcanic
islands. The majority of its people live clustered close to the coasts.

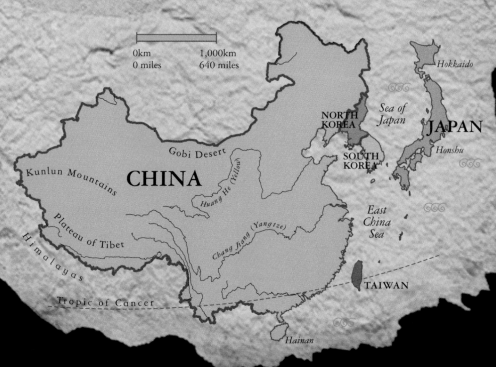

0km   1,000km
0 miles   640 miles

Hokkaido

NORTH
KOREA

Sea of
Japan

JAPAN

Honshu

SOUTH
KOREA

Gobi Desert

Kunlun Mountains

CHINA

Huang He (Yellow)

East
China
Sea

Plateau of Tibet

Chang Jiang (Yangtze)

Himalayas

TAIWAN

Tropic of Cancer

Hainan

Threatened environments

The Yangtze

The River Yangtze snakes across the huge country of China, from the high Plateau of Tibet in the west to the city of Shanghai on the eastern coast. It is the longest river in Asia and the third longest river in the world. The Yangtze provides a vital travel link between many of China's cities, and each day hundreds of thousands of ships transport people and goods along it.

An enormous concrete dam has been built across the Yangtze, to generate electricity for millions of homes, control flooding and allow ships to reach even more cities upriver. However, many people all over the world are opposed to the dam, and think it will damage the environment.

The River Yangtze flows through several gorges lined with steep, rocky cliffs. This ship is entering the Xiling Gorge.

These built-up areas, close to Mount Fuji in Japan, could be in danger if the volcano erupts in the future.

Mount Fuji

On a clear day, the snowy slopes of Mount Fuji are visible from Tokyo, Japan's capital city. Its beautiful, almost-symmetrical cone makes Mount Fuji one of the most famous volcanoes in the world. It is also the highest mountain in Japan, and thousands of adventurous people climb it every day, scrambling up the slopes through the night to reach the peak in time for sunrise.

Although the Japanese used to worship Mount Fuji, believing it to be home to a goddess, the volcano is now a potential threat to millions of homes. It last erupted around 300 years ago, and scientists believe that it could erupt again in the future, with disastrous results for the cities and towns nearby.

INTERNET LINK

For a link to a website where you can find out about the building of the Three Gorges Dam across the River Yangtze, go to **www.usborne-quicklinks.com**

42

Central China is home to endangered giant pandas. Their woodland homes can be destroyed when people cut down trees to clear farmland.

China's forests

The last giant pandas left in the wild live in the mist-shrouded mountain forests of central China. There are now only around 1,000 of these black-and-white bears left. Giant pandas eat the tender shoots of a kind of grass called bamboo, and they spend up to 16 hours every day searching for enough to eat. They are endangered because bamboo has been cut down in China to make space for farming.

China's desert

The Taklimakan Desert, in northwest China, is the second biggest sandy desert in the world. Conditions there are so harsh that many people have died trying to cross it. In the day, it is baking hot, but at night it is freezing cold. There are often sandstorms, and many deadly snakes live there. Millions of years ago, the Taklimakan Desert was a sea, and it is possible to find chunks of ancient coral there, among the rocks.

The mounds you can see either side of this man are the tops of buildings that were buried many years ago by the sands of the Taklimakan Desert.

43

Useful land

Industry in Taiwan

Many of Taiwan's factories produce plastics and dyes to be sold to other countries.

The island of Taiwan is remarkably pretty, with steep peaks towering over leafy forests. The country is too small to grow many crops or to have its own abundant natural resources, but it is known worldwide as a place for manufacturing and trade. All kinds of electronic and other goods are made there to be sold to other countries around the globe.

Crops in China

The River Yangtze roughly divides China's north and south. The main food crop in the cooler, drier north is wheat, which is made into noodles or boiled with water to make porridge. In southern China, the main food crop is rice. The warm, moist climate is ideal for rice, and when big rivers such as the Yangtze flood each year, they provide huge areas of rich farmland where it can grow. China produces more rice than any other country in the world, but most of this is used to feed southern China's growing population – hardly any is sold to other countries.

Rice fields need plenty of attention, but as hundreds of millions of people live in southern China, a supply of farm workers there is not a problem. These workers are planting young rice plants.

INTERNET LINK
For a link to a website about rice, Asia's most important food crop, with facts, figures and a description of life in a rice-growing family, go to **www.usborne-quicklinks.com**

River fishing

In parts of China and Japan, some river fishermen use birds called cormorants to help them catch fish. Each fisherman has several birds tied to his boat with twine. The twine is fastened to rings around the birds' necks, tight enough to keep them from swallowing fish. On a signal from the fishermen, the birds dive into the water and catch fish in their beaks, then bring them back to the boat. When fishing is over for the night, the rings are removed and the cormorants can eat.

A cormorant has dived underwater and managed to catch hold of this slippery fish in its beak.

Japanese springs

Japan has around 100 active volcanoes, and is also prone to earthquakes. But there are some benefits to living in such a volcanic region. All over Japan, there are hot springs, where volcanic activity heats the water and makes it pleasantly warm for bathing. People visit these hot springs, but they're not the only ones. Monkeys called snow macaques have discovered that the warm pools are good places to escape the freezing temperatures of Japan's bitterly cold winters.

This animal is a snow macaque. It is taking a dip in a volcanic hot pool, to warm itself up in the freezing cold of a Japanese winter.

45

Far Eastern style

Chinese cooking

Different parts of China have their own unique cooking styles. In southern areas, food is steamed in bamboo baskets and delicately seasoned. In the west, many dishes are spiced with hot chilies and pepper. Meat and vegetable dishes are usually served with rice in the south, but with noodles in the north. Lavish meals for special occasions are made up of a selection of dishes, picked to provide contrasting tastes, smells and textures.

This small dish of soy sauce is for dipping food in.

A Chinese meal often has several dishes served with rice or noodles. People help themselves, using chopsticks to pick up small pieces of food to eat with their rice or noodles.

Japanese homes

Many Japanese homes are built of wood and decorated simply, using natural materials. The floor is covered in thick *tatami* mats woven from straw. People sit on cushions on the floor, and sleep there too, on *futon* mattresses that are rolled up out of the way in the day. Sliding wood-and-paper *shoji* screens create separate rooms.

Light filters through paper screens into the dining room of this Japanese home.

INTERNET LINK

For a link to a website with information on life in Japan and recipes you can try, go to
www.usborne-quicklinks.com

Busy Chinese city

Hong Kong, in China, is one of the world's most crowded and exciting cities. It is squeezed onto an island, and land there is scarce and expensive. People live crammed into small apartments in high-rise blocks, and the skyline bristles with tall office skyscrapers. Many people choose to live on the nearby mainland or other islands, where there is more space.

In Hong Kong, in China, apartments, stores and offices crowd closely together.

Japanese clothes

Most Japanese people wear western-style clothes such as jeans, skirts and t-shirts. But for parties, weddings, visits to shrines and other special occasions, they often wear *kimonos*. A *kimono* is a wrap-around gown with flowing sleeves, fastened at the waist with a wide belt called an *obi*. Men, women and children all wear *kimonos*. Some *kimonos* are made of embroidered silk and are extremely valuable, but they can also be made of cheap, printed cotton. The style depends on who is wearing the *kimono*, what the occasion is and also on the time of year.

This girl is wearing a *kimono* for the Shichigosan festival, a Japanese celebration for girls aged 3 and 7, and boys aged 3 and 5.

Religions

Chinese New Year

The highlight of the Chinese calendar is the New Year festival. Families remember their ancestors with a feast on New Year's Eve. On New Year's Day, they eat vegetarian food, as the Chinese believe this will bring them a long, happy life. Around this time, people also light scented bamboo incense sticks and pray to their ancestors. The celebrations last for 15 days, building up to the Lantern Festival on the final night, when there are spectacular lantern displays and parades of people in fantastic costumes.

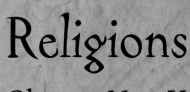

During the Andong Mask Dance Festival, people pay their respects to spirits by performing dances wearing masks like these.

Korean festivals

Some of Korea's many festivals are a chance for people to remember the ancient spirit world. Others are based on the teachings of Confucius, who encouraged people to worship their ancestors. Korean life is closely linked to farming, and so many of the festivals there are based on the seasons of the year and the harvest. But now, most South Koreans are Christian and celebrate Christmas and Easter, too.

A dancer holds up a spectacular dragon's head. He's taking part in a Dragon Dance, in Hong Kong, as part of the Chinese New Year celebrations.

INTERNET LINK

For a link to a website where you can learn more about the Chinese New Year festival, go to **www.usborne-quicklinks.com**

48

The Japanese spirit world

The Shinto religion is unique to Japan. Its followers believe that spirits called *kami* live in natural things, such as wind, mountains, rivers and trees. Shinto shrines are simple, peaceful places, often in a forest or by water, where people can be close to nature. At the entrance to a shrine is a gate called a *torii*, symbolizing the border between the human and the spirit worlds. Inside, people pray and make offerings to keep evil spirits away.

For followers of Shinto, these red pillars form gates that symbolize entry to the spirit world. The inscriptions are the names of the people who gave money for each gate.

Tibetan Buddhism

Tibet was once an independent country, with its own religion, a branch of Buddhism called *Vajrayana*. In 1950, Tibet became part of China. Religion was discouraged for many years, but now, Buddhism is once again a very visible part of life in Tibet, and monasteries that were closed have been re-opened. Many young boys spend some time in the monasteries, living as trainee monks called novices as part of their general education.

This boy is studying to be a monk at a Tibetan Buddhist monastery in Lhasa, Tibet's main city. Young monks study the Tibetan language and Buddhist teachings.

49

Art and entertainment

Japan's national sport

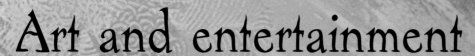

A Japanese *sumo* wrestler warms up before a fight. Behind him sit his opponent and the referee.

The traditional national sport of Japan is *sumo*, a form of wrestling, watched by millions at live matches or on TV. Two wrestlers called *rikishi* fight each other in a small ring. Each tries to push his opponent out of the ring, or force him to touch the floor with any part of the body apart from his feet. Most matches only last for a few seconds. *Rikishi* are highly respected in Japan, and wear special costumes even when they are not fighting, so that everyone can see they are *sumo* wrestlers.

Chinese opera

Opera has always been popular in China and Taiwan, and in the past it's even been used to send out political messages as well as to tell stories. Each performance is an entertaining blend of mime, dance, singing and swordfighting. The props used on stage are quite simple, such as an oar to show a boat, or a strip of ribbon to represent a river. Performances are accompanied by a small band of string and percussion players.

The mainly red costume of this Beijing Opera performer tells the audience that he is playing a loyal character.

This Chinese Buddhist monk is learning *kung fu* at Shaolin Temple, a place famous for the study of *kung fu*.

Martial arts

Martial arts are often regarded as sports but in fact they began as philosophies or ways of thinking, in Eastern Asia. Martial arts students learn skills of mind and body that they can use to defend themselves. Well-known martial arts include *judo* from Japan, *tae kwon do* from Korea and *kung fu* from China.

Kung fu began thousands of years ago, in central China. It uses kicking and punching techniques, and was made famous around the world in the 20th century by Bruce Lee, a movie star from Hong Kong.

Chinese calligraphy

Chinese calligraphy, or the art of writing, is based on the written Chinese language, and has also been adapted for the Japanese and Korean written languages. Written Chinese has thousands of characters, each of which is a symbol, formed by an intricate pattern of strokes, drawn in a particular order. Calligraphy is traditionally drawn using a brush and ink, and there are many different calligraphic styles, varying from spiky, separated and angular, to free-flowing and joined-up.

Chinese calligraphy is written from top to bottom, and from right to left. Water is added to a solid ink-block to make a pool of ink that the brush is dipped into.

INTERNET LINK

For a link to a website with an introduction to Japanese calligraphy, and a chance to try virtual calligraphy, go to **www.usborne-quicklinks.com**

A gigantic statue of the Buddha
(the founder of Buddhism) provides
a place for a young Buddhist monk
to sit in a park in Laos.

Mainland Southeast Asia

Burma (Myanmar), Thailand, Laos, Vietnam, Cambodia

In this book, Southeast Asia has been divided into Mainland Southeast Asia and Maritime Southeast Asia, which you can read about in the next section. Mainland Southeast Asia is made up of five countries that fit together, jigsaw-like, on a knob of land that juts out from the southeastern corner of Asia. The River Mekong flows through them all and forms natural borders between Laos and the countries of Burma (Myanmar) and Thailand.

All the countries share similar climates, with gently sloping landscapes covered in tropical forests and good farmland. Most people in these countries are followers of Buddhism, and it is usual to see Buddhist monks wandering the streets in their golden, saffron-dyed robes, and to spot the steeply sloping roofs of Buddhist temples poking up above the dark green foliage of the trees.

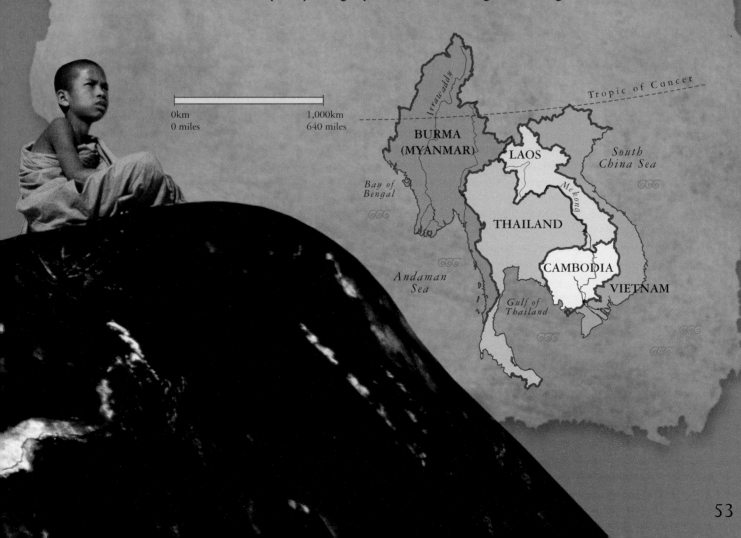

0km   1,000km
0 miles   640 miles

Tropic of Cancer

Irrawaddy

BURMA (MYANMAR)

LAOS

South China Sea

Bay of Bengal

Mekong

THAILAND

Andaman Sea

CAMBODIA

VIETNAM

Gulf of Thailand

Waterways and plantations

Linking countries

The River Mekong, which flows from China through Burma (Myanmar), Thailand, Laos, Cambodia and Vietnam, is the longest river in Southeast Asia. Boats can travel along much of the river's length, apart from a dangerous section in Cambodia near the Khone Falls.

The Mekong helps link the countries of Mainland Southeast Asia. Many of the 60 million people who live near the river are in small villages that can only be reached by boat. The countries in this region transport goods along the Mekong to trade with each other. They also use the river to transport goods to ports on the South China Sea, from where they can be traded with countries all over the world.

Cambodia's big lake

A net stretched between boats across a river helps these men catch fish swimming away from the shrinking Tonle Sap Lake in Cambodia.

The Tonle Sap, in Cambodia, is the biggest lake in Southeast Asia. It is connected to the large Mekong river by a much smaller river. In the dry season, the lake is shallow enough for a person to stand up in. But during the rainy season, it's over ten times deeper. This happens because the small river's flow changes direction twice each year. During the rainy season, the Mekong's floodwaters force water back up the small river into the lake, but in the dry season the river flows the other way, and the lake's waters sink again.

Here you can see part of the River Mekong flowing through Laos. It's the rainy season, and the river is very full of sediment washed from the land, which makes it look pinkish-brown.

Thousands of small, limestone islands like these are scattered across the still waters of Halong Bay, in northern Vietnam.

Vietnam's dragon

Southeast Asia has some incredibly dramatic coastlines. Halong Bay, in Vietnam, curves around the northwestern corner of the South China Sea. It is studded with over 3,000 small islands jutting out of the calm waters.

The islands form fantastic shapes, and their silhouettes inspire names such as Dragon Island and Man's Head Island. Some are hollow, their insides carved out by sea water to form caves. A Vietnamese legend tells that Halong Bay and its many scattered islands were formed when a giant dragon landed, and swished its massive tail from side to side in the sea.

INTERNET LINK

For a link to a website where you can take a photographic tour of the River Mekong region in the south of Vietnam, go to **www.usborne-quicklinks.com**

Coconuts in Thailand

In the wild, the seeds from coconut palms drift on the sea to places where new plants can take root. This is why the beaches in many hot countries are fringed by coconut palms. But products from coconut palms are very useful, and so many farmers in hot countries such as Thailand cultivate large crops of them in plantations. Coconuts can be eaten raw, and are also used in cooking. Even the hairy outer husks are used to make brushes and sacks.

These men are removing the outer husks from freshly picked coconuts, on the island of Koh Samui in southern Thailand. Each coconut palm can produce up to 100 coconuts every year.

Hard workers

Gold from the Mekong

Many Buddhist temples in Southeast Asia are adorned with gold decorations and statues coated in paper-thin gold leaf. People rub gold leaf onto parts of temples or statues of the Buddha (the founder of Buddhism) as a sign of respect.

People search in the River Mekong for gold to sell. There is gold in the mud and rocks of the riverbed, which is stirred up by the flowing water. People use wooden pans to pick through the mud for flecks and nuggets of gold. The money they earn can help them buy expensive items such as farm equipment.

There are small amounts of gold in the muddy Mekong riverbed. This woman from Laos is trying to sift out specks of gold using a shallow pan.

Working elephants

Southeast Asia is home to thousands of Asian elephants. In Thailand, most are trained to work, either hauling logs from felled trees or carrying tourists on treks. Each working elephant has its own keeper, who trains and feeds it.

As forests are cut down in Thailand, the areas where elephants can live shrink. Many keepers bring their elephants to cities such as Bangkok to work, but it's hard to find enough food for their elephants there.

This young working elephant is being washed by its trainer at an elephant hospital in Thailand.

Fishing on Lake Inle

A fisherman stands on the back of his boat on Lake Inle. From here, he can easily see fish swimming in the lake's waters.

Lake Inle, in Burma (Myanmar), is home to the Intha people. They use a unique method called leg-rowing to get around the lake on their boats. A fisherman stands at the back of his narrow, flat boat on one leg, and wraps the other leg around his long oar, pushing back with his calf to propel the boat forward. This leaves one hand free for him to move the conical bamboo trap into position to net fish.

When the fisherman becomes tired, he can switch to rowing with his other leg.

INTERNET LINK

For a link to a website with a visual introduction to the difficulties faced by the people of Burma (Myanmar), go to **www.usborne-quicklinks.com**

Water buffaloes

Many farmers in Southeast Asia use water buffaloes to work on rice fields and move heavy logs. Buffaloes cope with the hot climate by taking frequent dips in rivers or swamps to coat themselves in mud, which protects them from the burning sun and biting insects. But the buffaloes' role is threatened by modern farm machinery. Unlike buffaloes, machinery doesn't need a break during the hottest part of the day.

Two water buffaloes pull a farm cart in the hills of Thailand. Asian farmers have used buffaloes for over 2,000 years, and the animals are very precious to them. The buffaloes sleep near the house, guarded by the family dogs.

Village and city life

Mountain people

In the past, many people journeyed from China and Tibet to settle in the hills of Southeast Asia. Today, descendants of these people still live in the northern hills of Thailand, Vietnam, Burma (Myanmar) and Laos, as well as southern China. The groups all have different spoken languages, traditions, religions and styles of clothing. Many tourists visit their villages to see their ways of life. Some people think this threatens the villagers and treats them unfairly, but others argue that it brings money to the communities.

This Padaung woman lives in Thailand. For most of her life she has worn brass rings around her neck, which push her shoulders down, making her neck look longer.

Working villages

In many villages in Southeast Asia, all the villagers concentrate on making one particular product. This means they can produce large quantities of things to sell, such as carved wooden furniture, paper umbrellas or incense sticks – short slivers of perfumed bamboo designed to be burned slowly. Millions of incense sticks are used in the region every day for religious ceremonies, so they are always in demand. A single incense factory worker can make up to 15,000 sticks in one day.

This Vietnamese girl makes incense sticks by rolling strips of bamboo in fine sawdust. She adds perfume, then leaves the sticks to dry.

Bustling Bangkok

Bangkok, the capital city of Thailand, is one of the biggest and busiest cities in Southeast Asia. It is built on the banks of the Chao Phraya river, and is criss-crossed with a network of canals, called *khlongs*, which are teeming with small boats. The wide city streets seethe with traffic jams and the hot, damp air is thick with exhaust fumes.

But Bangkok is also famous for its glittering golden spires, richly ornamented palaces and secluded temples. A famous, old temple in Bangkok is Wat Pho, home of one of the largest Buddha images in Thailand.

This huge golden statue of the Buddha is in one of Bangkok's temples, Wat Pho. The soles of the feet are inlaid with mother-of-pearl designs, including 108 pictures of the Buddha at different stages of his life.

INTERNET LINK

For a link to a website where you can see stunning photographs of some of Bangkok's many temples, go to **www.usborne-quicklinks.com**

Incredible temples

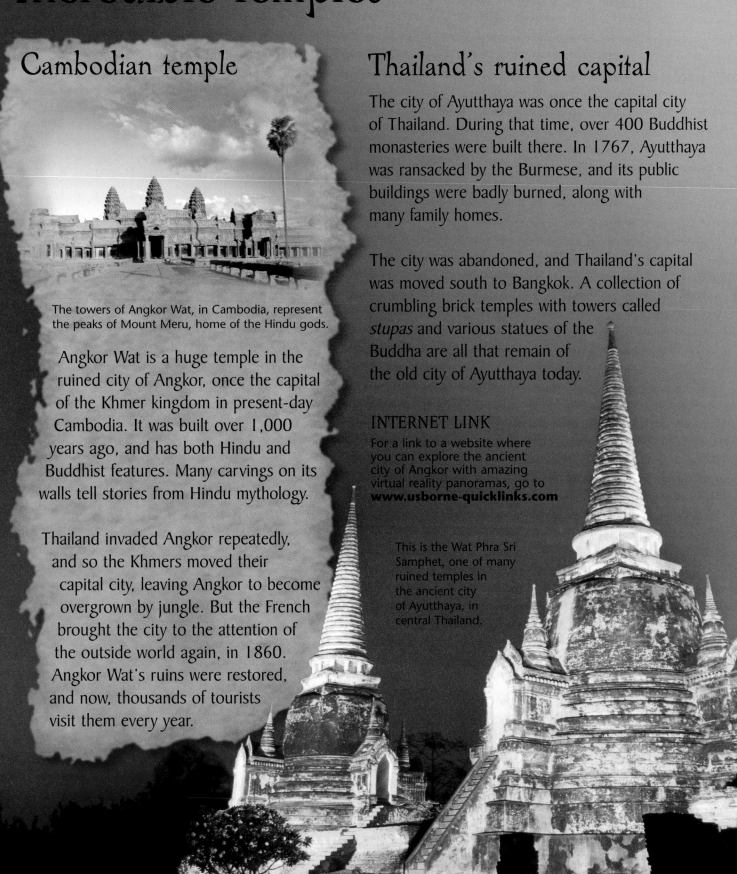

Cambodian temple

The towers of Angkor Wat, in Cambodia, represent the peaks of Mount Meru, home of the Hindu gods.

Angkor Wat is a huge temple in the ruined city of Angkor, once the capital of the Khmer kingdom in present-day Cambodia. It was built over 1,000 years ago, and has both Hindu and Buddhist features. Many carvings on its walls tell stories from Hindu mythology.

Thailand invaded Angkor repeatedly, and so the Khmers moved their capital city, leaving Angkor to become overgrown by jungle. But the French brought the city to the attention of the outside world again, in 1860. Angkor Wat's ruins were restored, and now, thousands of tourists visit them every year.

Thailand's ruined capital

The city of Ayutthaya was once the capital city of Thailand. During that time, over 400 Buddhist monasteries were built there. In 1767, Ayutthaya was ransacked by the Burmese, and its public buildings were badly burned, along with many family homes.

The city was abandoned, and Thailand's capital was moved south to Bangkok. A collection of crumbling brick temples with towers called *stupas* and various statues of the Buddha are all that remain of the old city of Ayutthaya today.

INTERNET LINK

For a link to a website where you can explore the ancient city of Angkor with amazing virtual reality panoramas, go to **www.usborne-quicklinks.com**

This is the Wat Phra Sri Samphet, one of many ruined temples in the ancient city of Ayutthaya, in central Thailand.

Cambodian dancers wear ornate gold and silk costumes. The designs have hardly changed for hundreds of years.

Temple dancers

Traditional Cambodian dances are performed in temples, and often tell religious stories. The dancers are beautiful young girls, who represent *apsaras*, or heavenly beings. Their moves are flowing and graceful and the dancers wear tranquil smiles. Originally, the dances were performed for royalty and monks.

Famous golden rock

One of the most sacred Buddhist sites in Burma (Myanmar) is Kyaiktiyo Paya, the Golden Rock Pagoda. Most Burmese people try to visit it at least once in their lifetime. The pagoda is perched on top of a huge rock coated with gold leaf, precariously balanced on the edge of a cliff. People believe there is one of the Buddha's hairs inside the pagoda, and that this keeps the boulder from tumbling down the mountainside. Sometimes the rock sways, but it never quite falls.

Devoted visitors to Kyaiktiyo Paya in Burma (Myanmar) crowd close to the golden rock. Only men are allowed to touch it.

61

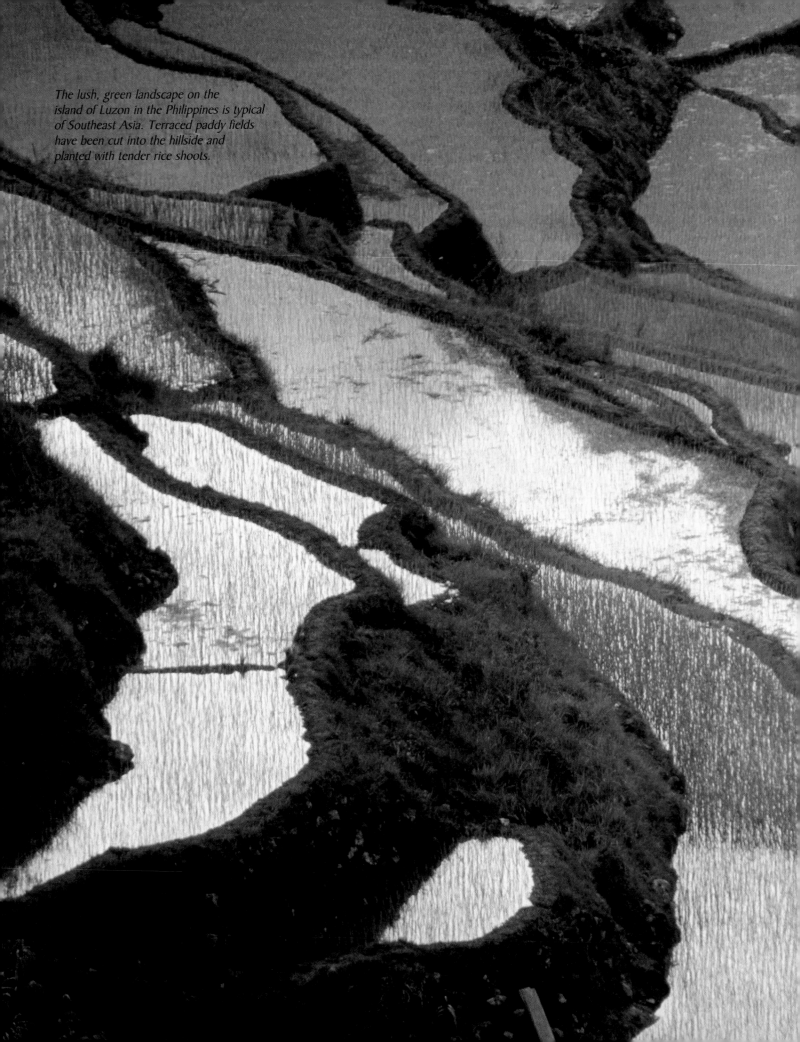

The lush, green landscape on the
island of Luzon in the Philippines is typical
of Southeast Asia. Terraced paddy fields
have been cut into the hillside and
planted with tender rice shoots.

Maritime Southeast Asia

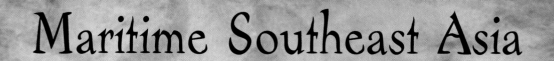

Malaysia, Singapore, Indonesia, Brunei, Philippines, East Timor

Maritime means "near the sea". The lower part of Southeast Asia is sometimes given this name because it is made up of over 24,000 islands and much of its land is close to the sea. Indonesia alone has over 17,000 islands, stretching from Sumatra in the west, as far as New Guinea in the east. Only the western part of the island of New Guinea belongs to the Asian country of Indonesia; the island is usually considered part of Oceania.

The long coastlines of Maritime Southeast Asia are lapped by tropical seas. Most of this area is hot and the air is extremely damp, except for a few of Indonesia's rockier islands, which are quite dry. Many of the islands are covered in rainforest and the larger ones are mountainous. Indonesia also has hundreds of volcanoes, many of which are active.

Wild living

Volcanoes of Indonesia

Indonesia has more active volcanoes than any other country in the world, running along the length of its main islands. The most active volcano in Indonesia today is Merapi, on the island of Java. But the largest volcanic eruption in recorded history may have been when Tambora erupted on the island of Sumbawa, in 1815. Ash fell on many Indonesian islands up to 1,300km (800 miles) away, and blocked out the Sun's light, causing unusually cold weather around the world.

The cone-shaped mounds you can see here are active and extinct volcanoes in Indonesia. The steaming crater on the left is Mount Bromo.

Rainforest wildlife

Tropical forests cover large areas of Indonesia and are home to a variety of rare animal species, including Sumatran tigers, long-snouted Malayan tapirs and large apes, such as long-armed silvery gibbons.

Many apes hardly ever come down to the ground. Instead, they use their strong limbs to swing through the branches of trees. The apes that live in the wild in Southeast Asia are becoming endangered as trees are cut down in the forests where they live. But some of the areas are now protected national parks.

This young orangutan is hanging in a tree in Tanjung Puting National Park on Sumatra, a large Indonesian island.

INTERNET LINK

For a link to a website about the terrifying waves that can occur as a result of earthquakes and volcanic eruptions, go to **www.usborne-quicklinks.com**

The swirling cloud above is a storm called a typhoon approaching the islands of the Philippines (shown with outlines) in April 2003.

Isolated island creatures

Many of Southeast Asia's islands are havens for rare creatures that don't exist in the wild in other parts of the world. The hot, rocky island of Komodo, in Indonesia, is home to the world's largest lizard, the Komodo dragon. Groups of dragons also live on the nearby islands of Rinca, Padar and Flores, but it is still considered to be an endangered species. This is because the dragons live in a relatively small area of the world, and a single natural disaster such as a volcanic eruption could wipe out every single one.

Stormy Philippines

The mountainous islands of the Philippines take the full, frightening force of tropical storms called typhoons, that sweep in from the Pacific Ocean to the east. Around 20 typhoons hit the Philippines every year, lashing the islands with torrential rain, and winds strong enough to blow people off their feet. People are killed by typhoons in the Philippines each year, and they also cause terrible wind damage, flattening buildings and crops. The heavy rains cause water levels to rise suddenly, and there are often devastating flash floods and mudslides. Even after a storm has passed, there are dangers from damaged electricity cables and diseases spread by a lack of fresh water.

A bite from a Komodo dragon like this one can seriously injure a person. The mouths of these giant lizards contain deadly germs.

Farming and environment

Rice terraces

Rice is Asia's main food, so it is grown in many Asian countries with climates that are warm, wet and sunny enough. The steamy, tropical climates of the Philippines and Indonesia are ideal for growing rice, but much of the farmland in these countries is extremely hilly. So they can grow rice on the hillsides, farmers dig out flat terraces in the land. These keep the water the rice needs from washing away. Other hill farmers grow rice dry, which means it doesn't need to stand in water.

Rice grows on terraced farmland in Indonesia. The plants stand in a layer of water, which helps them grow and makes it easier for the farmers to control weeds.

Sugar cane

A man collects sugar cane to take to a factory, where it will be turned into sugar.

Sugar cane is a very useful crop that grows in Indonesia and the Philippines, as well as other tropical countries around the world. It's a type of giant grass, almost all of which can be used for food. The stems are squeezed to drain the juice out and then boiled, to leave grains of sugar. Any pulpy leftovers are used to make animal feed. Liquid from the pressed sugar cane also makes a sweet, refreshing drink.

Cash crops

Much of Southeast Asia's land is used to grow crops that don't feed the local population, but are turned into products that can be sold to other countries. These are sometimes called cash crops. Cash crops that grow in this region include sugar cane, rubber, and spices such as pepper.

Rubber trees grow extremely well in the warm, moist climates of Indonesia and Malaysia, and many farmers there plant them in closely-spaced rows. Rubber is made from a liquid called latex that gathers beneath the bark of the tree. Farmers cut sloping grooves in the bark of the rubber trees and collect the latex that trickles out.

INTERNET LINK

For a link to a website where you can explore Borneo's rainforest at night and discover the animals that live there, go to **www.usborne-quicklinks.com**

A small cup is attached to the trunk of a rubber tree to catch the white latex that runs out. This is used to make rubber.

Forests in danger

Southeast Asia's lush rainforests are threatened by the cutting down of trees for commercial logging and to make space for farming. There are also massive forest fires. Some fires happen naturally and actually help certain forest plants to reproduce. But people also start fires to clear large areas of forest quickly. During very dry seasons, these small, man-made fires can spread rapidly, resulting in huge, out-of-control blazes that destroy millions of trees, plants and forest creatures. Smoke from the very big fires can drift and cause dangerously poor air quality in cities far away. This can affect people's health and even make plane travel hazardous.

A rainforest is on fire in the Indonesian part of the island of Borneo. In 1998, smoke from these widespread forest fires in Indonesia drifted to Malaysia and caused terrible air pollution there.

Spiritual beliefs

Old and new religions

Today, the majority of people living in the Philippines and East Timor are Christians. But before European settlers introduced Christianity to the region around 450 years ago, the main religion there was ancestor worship. Now, many people perform traditional ancestor worship alongside Christianity and other world religions such as Islam and Buddhism.

This girl is preparing for a Philippine festival called *Dinagyang*, which celebrates the arrival of Christianity with loud music, bright costumes and dancing.

Influence of Islam

Indonesia, Malaysia and Brunei together contain more followers of Islam, or Muslims, than any other region in the world. There are also many Muslims living in Singapore and the Philippines, and as a result there are mosques all over this region. Mosques have distinctive rounded domes and towers called minarets, from which Muslims are called to prayer. Many non-religious buildings in this region have also been influenced by aspects of Islamic architecture.

The Ubudiah Mosque is one of the most famous mosques in Malaysia. The towers each have space at the top for a man called a *muezzin* to call Muslims to prayer.

Balinese Hinduism

Indian traders brought Hinduism to Southeast Asia hundreds of years ago, and many people in Indonesia still follow the religion today, particularly on the small island of Bali. Balinese Hinduism has adapted to fit the island's way of life, with its own unique gods, goddesses and ceremonies. The island is covered in temples and shrines, the holiest of which is Besakih, on the slopes of Mount Agung, one of Bali's volcanoes. Dances are often performed by young girls in elaborate costumes to accompany the religious ceremonies that take place in the temples.

A young Balinese *Legong* dancer wears a costume decorated with gold, embroidery and fresh flowers. Many varieties of *Legong* tell the story of a beautiful princess.

INTERNET LINK

For a link to a website where you can take an amazing virtual tour of sites in Indonesia, including a Buddhist temple and a national park, go to **www.usborne-quicklinks.com**

Old and new traditions

Dyed Indonesian cloth

Batik is the name for the Indonesian technique of dyeing patterned cloth using wax. To make *batik*, melted wax is trickled onto cloth, making delicate shapes of lines and dots. The cloth is then dipped into dye. Wherever there is wax on the cloth, the dye doesn't soak in, and in this way a pattern forms. After the first dye bath, the wax is scraped off and new patterns are applied. The cloth is dyed again, to build up a more complicated design.

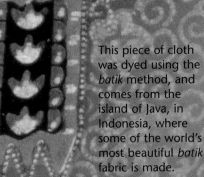

This piece of cloth was dyed using the *batik* method, and comes from the island of Java, in Indonesia, where some of the world's most beautiful *batik* fabric is made.

Malaysian skyscrapers

The Petronas Towers, in Malaysia's capital city, Kuala Lumpur, are among the tallest buildings in the world. The towers are occupied mainly by offices, but are also part of a development containing stores, a concert hall and a park. Each tower has 88 floors and is topped by a slim spire, and the two towers are joined by a bridge halfway up, which is open for the public to visit. Malaysia is a mainly Muslim country, and so the design of the towers was strongly influenced by Islamic architecture. They look rather like the minarets on top of a mosque.

The Petronas Towers, two of the world's tallest buildings, light up the skyline of Kuala Lumpur, capital city of Malaysia.

Singapore's mixture of styles

The tiny country of Singapore is home to people whose ancestors came to the island from all over Asia, as well as Europe. The styles of traditional architecture in Singapore have been influenced by the Chinese, Indians, Malays and British, or sometimes a mixture. Today there are also many modern, hi-tech office buildings and shopping malls.

Here you can see a row of Chinese-style buildings in Singapore, right in front of the island's biggest Muslim place of worship, the Sultan Mosque.

Indonesian puppets

Indonesian *wayang kulit* shadow puppet shows are performed against a cloth screen, lit from behind by a coconut oil lamp. They are based on long, famous Indian tales called the *Ramayana* and the *Mahabharata*. A single person controls over 20 different puppets, and he also provides all their voices, sings songs, and signals to the orchestra behind him to tell them what to play. Some shows are very long and the puppeteer may have to sit cross-legged for many hours.

An Indonesian shadow puppet like this one is made of a piece of leather, cut into intricate, lacy patterns.

INTERNET LINK

For a link to a website with a behind-the-screen look at Indonesian shadow puppets and clips of Indonesian music, go to **www.usborne-quicklinks.com**

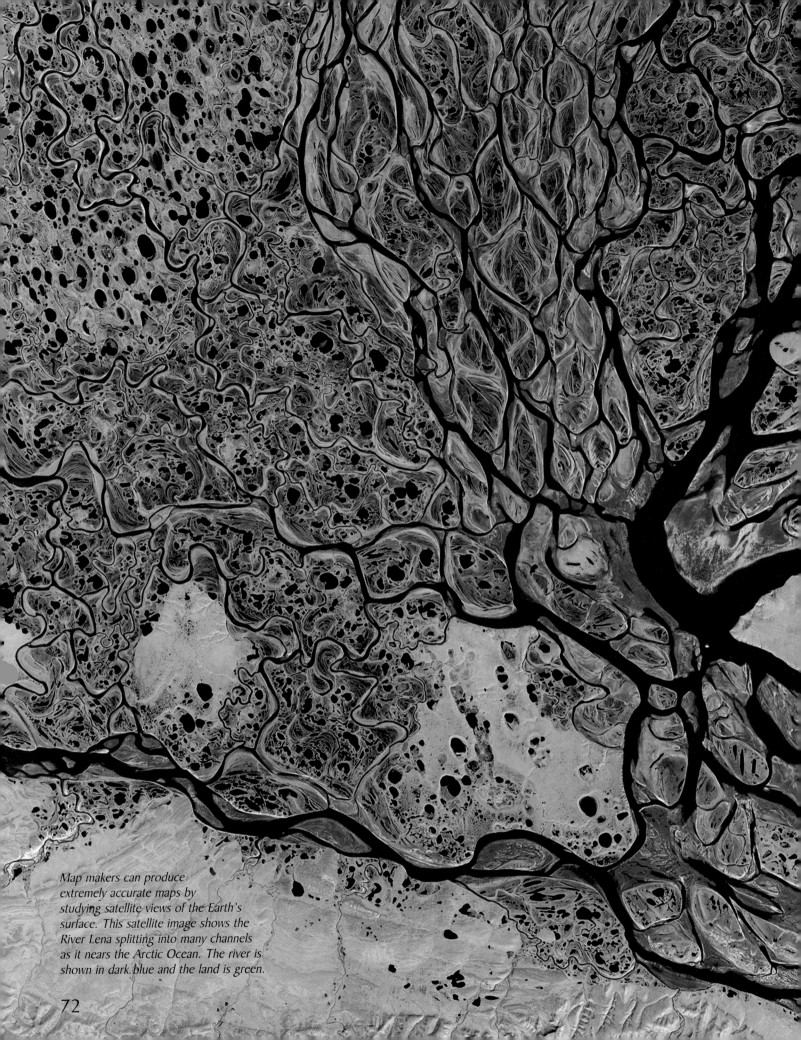

Map makers can produce extremely accurate maps by studying satellite views of the Earth's surface. This satellite image shows the River Lena splitting into many channels as it nears the Arctic Ocean. The river is shown in dark blue and the land is green.

Maps of Asia

On the following pages you can see environmental maps of Asia which show different types of landscape such as desert, mountain and forest. They also show borders between countries, as well as capital cities and other major cities and towns.

North is at the top of every map. The grid lines on the maps are latitude and longitude lines, measured in degrees (°) and minutes (´). These lines are used to pinpoint the exact location of any spot on the Earth's surface. Latitude lines run around the globe, or side-to-side on a map. Important lines of latitude are named, such as the equator (0°), the Tropic of Cancer (23°27´N) and the Arctic Circle (66°30´N). Lines of longitude run from north to south, or from top to bottom on a map.

The maps have numbered and lettered grids. If you look up a place or feature in the map index on page 90, you will find page numbers and grid references to help you find it on a map. All the maps have scale bars to tell you the real distance that is represented by a distance on the map. Each map also has a key to explain the shading and symbols.

Here is an explanation of the different kinds of land cover shown by the map keys:

Boreal forest is cold forest, also called *taiga*. It's made up mainly of evergreen trees.

Temperate forest has a cool and a warm season, and trees there seasonally lose all their leaves.

Tropical forest is found near the equator. It's always hot there, with rain nearly every day.

Temperate grassland has a cool season and a warm season. Few trees grow there.

Savanna is hot grassland that receives very little rain, and so there are hardly any trees.

Semi-desert and scrub is a dry zone where only a few small bushes and plants can grow.

Hot desert has scarcely any rain at all, and may be covered in sand, gravel or rock.

Wetland is covered in marsh or swamp, and is often flooded or waterlogged.

Mountain is very high, rocky land. Many peaks together form mountain ranges.

Tundra is land where the ground is frozen nearly all year round and no trees grow.

Ice can be either land with a permanent ice cap, or enormous sheets of sea ice.

Cultivation is land used for farming, where people grow crops or keep animals.

ARCTIC

Svalbard
(Norway)

A
B
C
D
E

Franz Josef
Land

North
Sea

Norwegian
Sea

Arctic Circle

North Cape

Murmansk

Barents
Sea

Novaya
Zemlya

Kola
Peninsula

Kara
Sea

UNITED
KINGDOM
London

Paris
BELGIUM
NETHERLANDS
LUXEMBOURG
FRANCE

NORWAY
Oslo

DENMARK

SWEDEN

Stockholm

FINLAND

Helsinki

Baltic
Sea

St. Petersburg

Arkhangelsk

Lake
Ladoga

Lake
Onega

Vorkuta

Norilsk

GERMANY

Berlin

CZECH
REPUBLIC
AUSTRIA

POLAND
Warsaw

SLOVAKIA

Budapest
HUNGARY

LITHUANIA
LATVIA
Vilnius
ESTONIA

BELARUS
Minsk

Lviv

Cherepovets

Ukhta

Novyy Urengoy

West Siberian
Plain

ROMANIA
MOLDOVA
Chisinau

Kiev
UKRAINE

Moscow

Ryazan

Nizhniy Novgorod

Kazan

Perm

Ob

Ural Mountains

Surgut

Yenisey

Ob

Kharkiv

Voronezh

Volga

Odesa
Dnipropetrovsk

Simferopol

Black
Sea

Rostov

Volgograd

Krasnodar

Samara

Oral

Orenburg

Yekaterinburg

Chelyabinsk

Omsk

Irtysh

R U S

Tomsk

Krasnoyarsk

Ankara

TURKEY

Adana

Mount Elbrus
5,642m
(18,510ft)
Astrakhan

GEORGIA

Tbilisi

ARMENIA
Yerevan

AZERBAIJAN
Baku

Caspian
Sea

Volga

Aqtobe

Atyrau

Aqtau

KAZAKHSTAN

Astana

Pavlodar

Qaraghandy

Novosibirsk

Barnaul

Abaka

Kyzyl

Aleppo

SYRIA

Mosul

Tabriz

Aral
Sea

Nukus

Qyzylorda

Balqash

Lake
Balkhash

Uskemen

Altay

Baghdad

IRAQ

Tehran
Damavand
5,604m
(18,386ft)

Ashgabat
(Ashkhabad)

TURKMENISTAN

Dasoguz

UZBEKISTAN

Shymkent

Tashkent

Samarqand

Almaty

Bishkek
KYRGYZSTAN
Osh

Tien Shan

Urumqi

Aksu

Tarim Basin

Altai

Ahvaz

Esfahan

Turkmenabat

Dushanbe
TAJIKISTAN

Kuwait City
KUWAIT

SAUDI
ARABIA

Shiraz

IRAN

Mashhad

Herat

Mazar-e Sharif

Taklimakan Desert

Hotan

Riyadh

Manama

QATAR

Doha

Abu Dhabi

Persian Gulf (The Gulf)

Bandar-e
Abbas

Zahedan

Kandahar

AFGHANISTAN

Kabul

Islamabad

K2
8,611m
(28,251ft)

PAKISTAN

Lahore

Srinagar

INDIA

Plateau of Tibet

Indus

60°
2
80°
20°
40°
60°
80°
1

3

40°
N

4

74

60°E
C
D
60°E
80°E
E

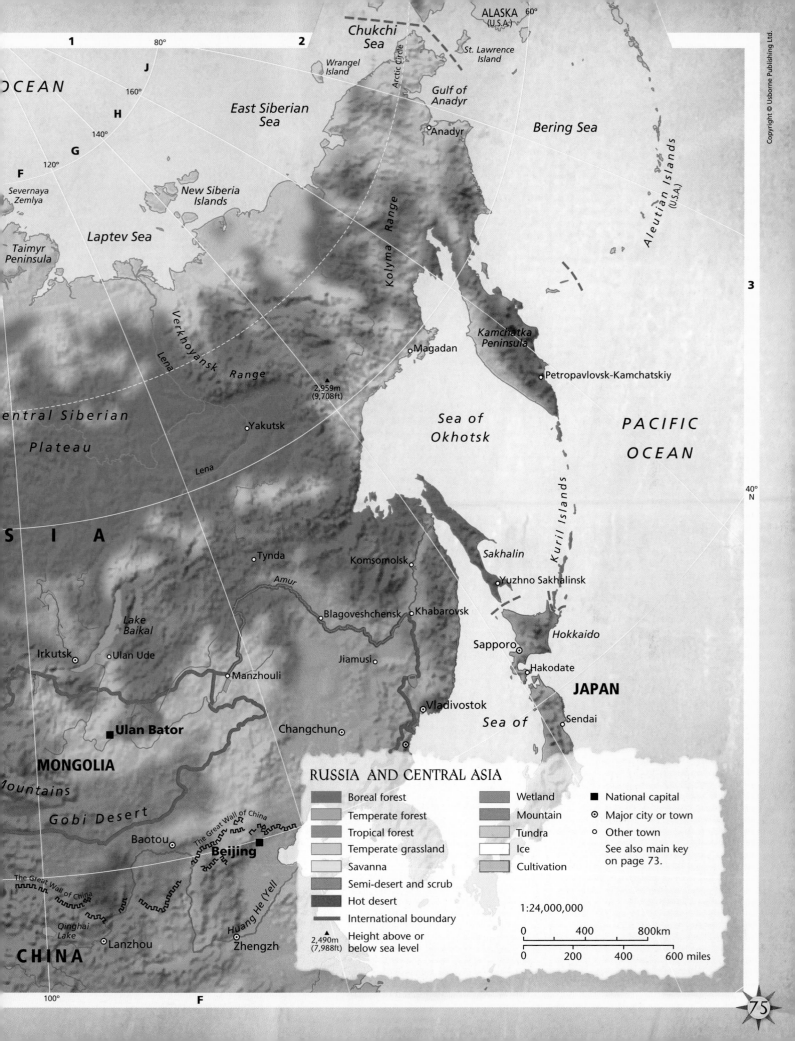

ALASKA (U.S.A.)   60°

Chukchi Sea

J

160°

Wrangel Island

St. Lawrence Island

H

140°

East Siberian Sea

Arctic Circle

Gulf of Anadyr

Bering Sea

G

120°

OCEAN

F

Severnaya Zemlya

New Siberia Islands

⊙ Anadyr

Aleutian Islands (U.S.A.)

Taimyr Peninsula

Laptev Sea

Verkhoyansk

3

Kolyma Range

Kamchatka Peninsula

⊙ Magadan

entral Siberian

Lena

2,959m (9,708ft)

⊙ Petropavlovsk-Kamchatskiy

Plateau

▲

Range

⊙ Yakutsk

Sea of Okhotsk

PACIFIC

Lena

OCEAN

40° N

S I A

Kuril Islands

⊙ Tynda

Komsomolsk ⊙

Sakhalin

⊙ Yuzhno Sakhalinsk

Amur

Lake Baikal

Blagoveshchensk ⊙ ⊙ Khabarovsk

Hokkaido

Irkutsk ⊙   ⊙ Ulan Ude

Jiamusi ⊙

Sapporo ⊙

⊙ Manzhouli

⊙ Hakodate

JAPAN

■ **Ulan Bator**

Changchun ⊙

⊙ Vladivostok

⊙ Sendai

MONGOLIA

Sea of

ountains

Gobi Desert

The Great Wall of China

Baotou ⊙

The Great Wall of China

Beijing ■

Qinghai Lake

Huang He (Yell

⊙ Lanzhou

Zhengzh

CHINA

100°   F

RUSSIA AND CENTRAL ASIA

▨ Boreal forest	▨ Wetland
▨ Temperate forest	▨ Mountain
▨ Tropical forest	▨ Tundra
▨ Temperate grassland	☐ Ice
▨ Savanna	▨ Cultivation
▨ Semi-desert and scrub	
▨ Hot desert	
— International boundary	

■ National capital

⊙ Major city or town

○ Other town

See also main key on page 73.

▲ 2,490m (7,988ft) Height above or below sea level

1:24,000,000

0	400	800km

0	200	400	600 miles

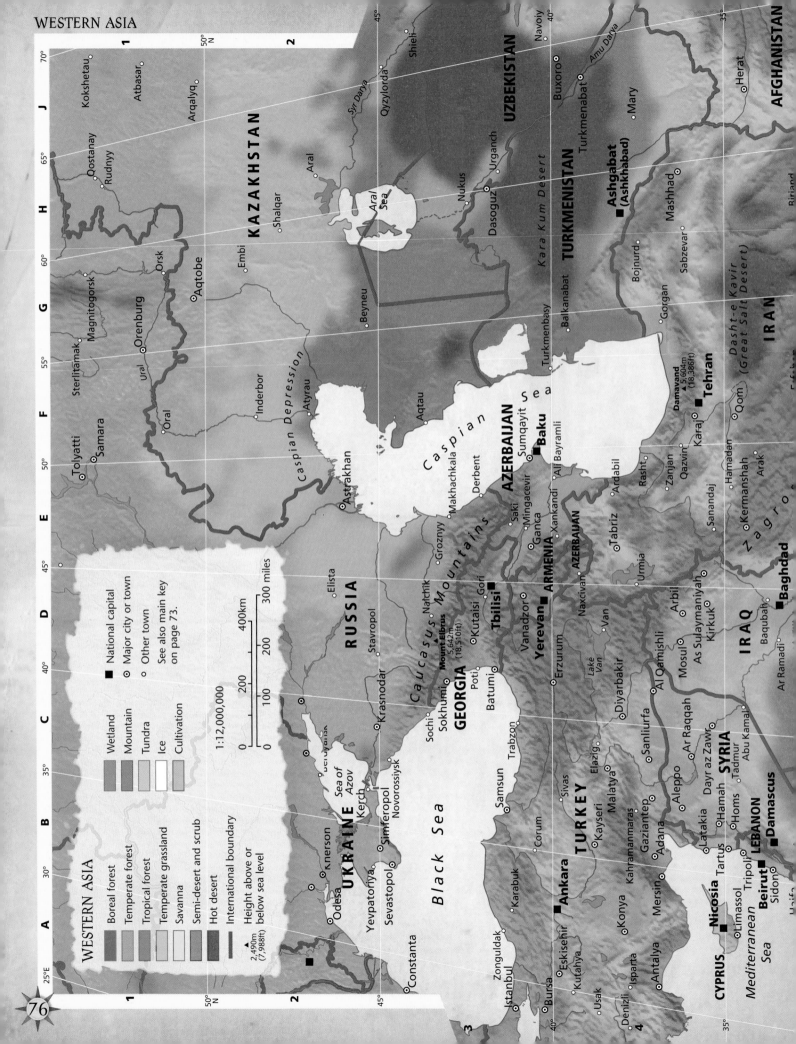

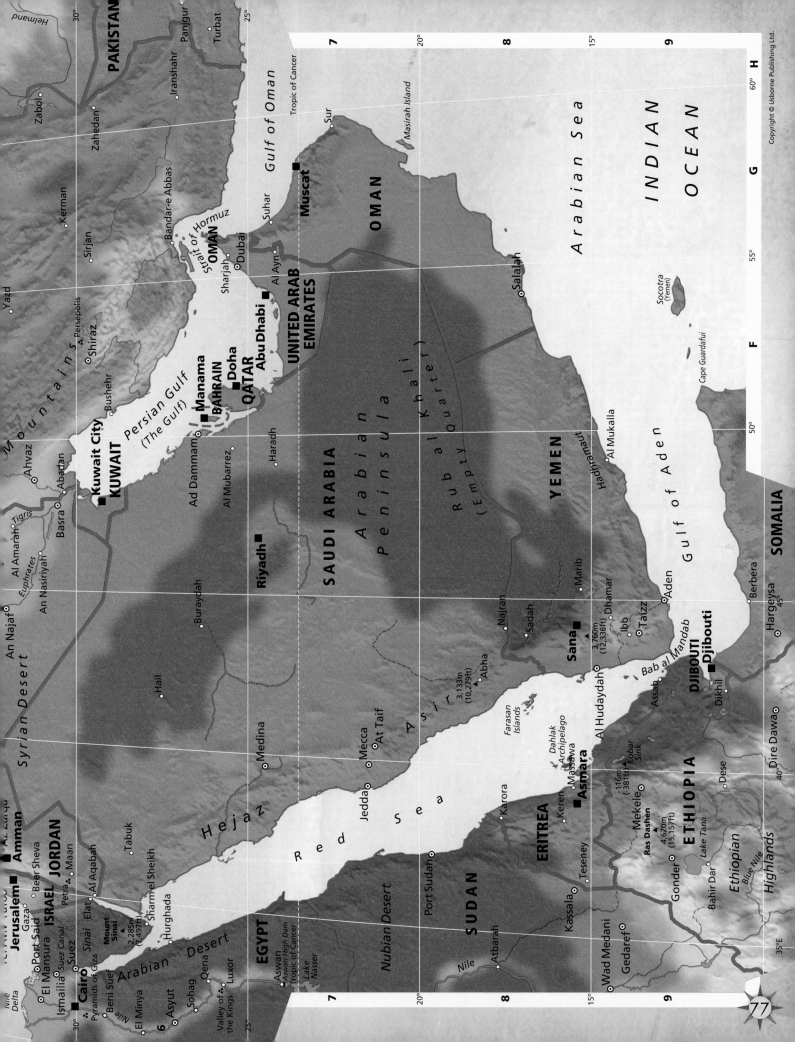

PAKISTAN

Zabol

30°

Helmand

Zahedan

Iranshahr

Panjgur

Turbat

25°

Tropic of Cancer

Gulf of Oman

Masirah Island

Sur

OMAN

Arabian Sea

INDIAN

Kerman

Sirjan

Bandar-e Abbas

Strait of Hormuz

Suhar

Muscat

OMAN

Yazd

Shiraz

Persepolis

Shiraz

Bushehr

Sharjah

Dubai

Al Ayn

OCEAN

Mountains

UNITED ARAB

EMIRATES

Socotra
(Yemen)

55°

F

Ahvaz

Abadan

Manama
BAHRAIN

Doha

Abu Dhabi

Salalah

Cape Guardafui

Persian Gulf
(The Gulf)

QATAR

Tigris

Kuwait City

Ad Dammam

Al Mubarrez

Haradh

Arabian

Peninsula

Rub al Khali
(Empty Quarter)

YEMEN

Al Mukalla

Gulf of Aden

50°

Basra

KUWAIT

Al Amarah

An Nasiriyah

Euphrates

An Najaf

An Nasiriyah

SAUDI ARABIA

Riyadh

Hadhramaut

SOMALIA

Buraydah

Najran

Sadah

Marib

Aden

Berbera

Syrian Desert

Hail

Abha

3,133m
(10,279ft)

Sana

3,760m
(12,336ft)

Dhamar

Ibb

Taizz

Bab al Mandab

DJIBOUTI

Djibouti

Hargeysa

45°

Amman

Al Zarqa

JORDAN

Beer Sheva

Maan

Tabuk

Medina

Mecca

At Taif

Asir

Farasan
Islands

Al Hudaydah

Assab

Dikhil

Kobar
Sink

Dire Dawa

ISRAEL

Jerusalem

Gaza

Petra

Al Aqabah

Jedda

Red Sea

Dahlak
Archipelago

Massawa

-116m
(-381ft)

Mekele

DJIBOUTI

Dese

Port Said

Beni Suef

Elat

Sinai

Sharm el Sheikh

Hejaz

Karora

Keren

Asmara

ERITREA

Ras Dashen
4,620m
(15,157ft)

ETHIOPIA

Ethiopian

El Mansura

Cairo

Pyramids of Giza

Mount
Sinai
2,285m
(7,497ft)

Hurghada

Teseney

Kassala

Gonder

Lake Tana

Bahir Dar

Highlands

Ismailia

Suez Canal

Suez

Qena

Luxor

Valley of
the Kings

Arabian

Desert

Nubian Desert

Port Sudan

SUDAN

Wad Medani

Gedaref

Blue Nile

40°

Nile

Delta

El Minya

Asyut

Sohag

EGYPT

Aswan
Aswan High Dam
Tropic of Cancer

Lake
Nasser

Nile

Atbarah

35°E

7

20°

8

15°

9

H

G

F

60°

55°

Copyright © Usborne Publishing Ltd.

6

7

20°

8

15°

9

77

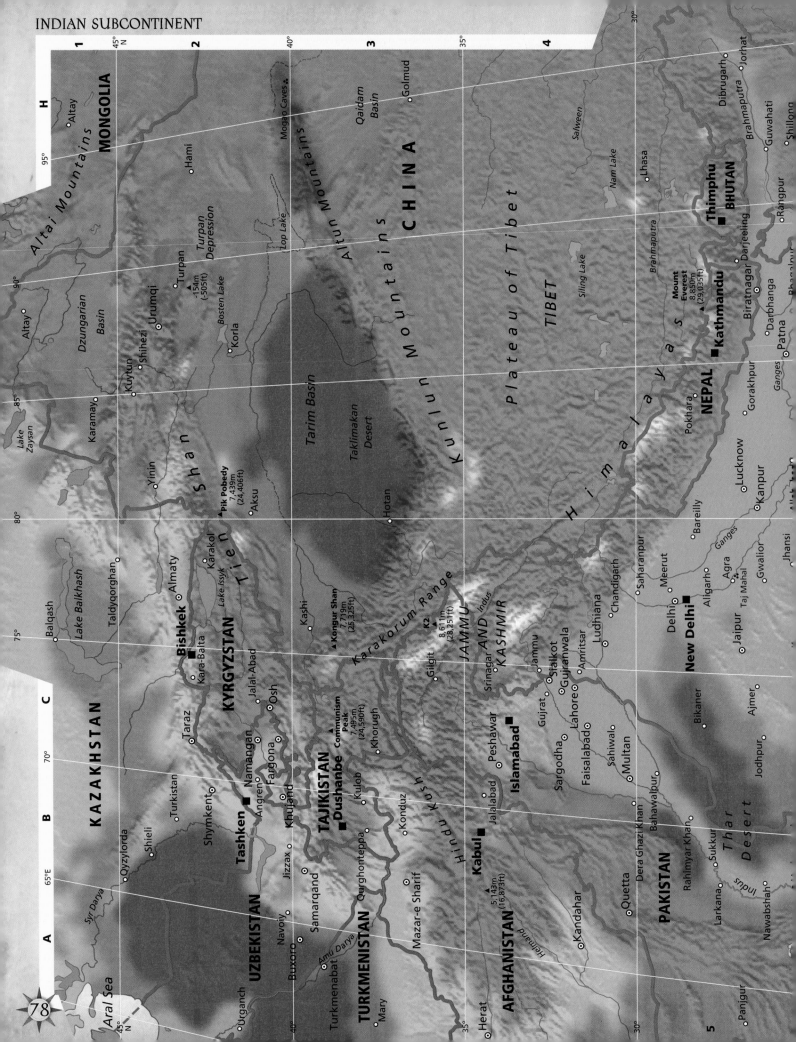

1   **2**   **3**   **4**

45° N   95°   90°   85°   80°   75°   70°   65°E

30°   35°

H

C

B

A

MONGOLIA

Altay

Altay

Hami

Altai Mountains

Lake Zaysan

Dzungarian Basin

Urumqi

Shihezi

Kuytun

Karamay

Yinin

T i e n S h a n

Turpan
Turpan Depression
-154m (-505ft)

Bosten Lake

Korla

Lop Lake

Mogo Caves

CHINA

Golmud

Qaidam Basin

Altun Mountains

Tarim Basin

Taklimakan Desert

Aksu

Pik Pobedy 7,439m (24,406ft)

Hotan

Kashi

Kongur Shan 7,719m (25,325ft)

K u n l u n M o u n t a i n s

Plateau of Tibet

TIBET

Salween

Nam Lake

Lhasa

Siling Lake

Brahmaputra

Mount Everest 8,850m (29,035ft)

Thimphu
BHUTAN

Kathmandu
NEPAL

Darjeeling
Biratnagar

Dibrugarh

Jorhat

Guwahati

Shillong

Rangpur

Brahmaputra

KAZAKHSTAN

Lake Balkhash

Balqash

Taldyqorghan

Almaty

Bishkek

Karakol

Lake Issyk

KYRGYZSTAN

Kara-Balta

Taraz

Jalal-Abad

Osh

Namangan

Fargona

Angren

Khujand

TAJIKISTAN

Dushanbe

Communism Peak 7,495m (24,590ft)

Khorugh

Kulob

Karakorum Range

K2 8,611m (28,251ft)

Gilgit

JAMMU AND KASHMIR

Srinagar

Indus

Jammu

Sialkot

Gujranwala

Amritsar

Ludhiana

Chandigarh

Jalandhar

Saharanpur

Meerut

Delhi
New Delhi

Aligarh
Agra
Taj Mahal

Jaipur

Ajmer

Bareilly

Gwalior

Jhansi

Lucknow

Kanpur

Gorakhpur

Ganges

Patna

Darbhanga

Ganges

Pokhara

Bikaner

Jodhpur

UZBEKISTAN

Qyzylorda

Shieli

Navoiy

Shymkent

Turkistan

Jizzax

Samarqand

Buxoro

Tashken

Ourghonteppa

Konduz

Mazar-e Sharif

TURKMENISTAN

Amu Darya

Syr Darya

Mary

Turkmenabat

Urganch

Aral Sea

45° N

Herat

Helmand

AFGHANISTAN

Kabul
5,143m (16,873ft)

Kandahar

Jalalabad

H i n d u K u s h

Peshawar

Islamabad

PAKISTAN

Quetta

Dera Ghazi Khan

Rahimyar Khan

Larkana

Sukkur

Nawabshah

Panjgur

Bahawalpur

Multan

Sahiwal

Faisalabad

Sargodha

Gujrat

Lahore

T h a r D e s e r t

Indus

H i m a l a y a s

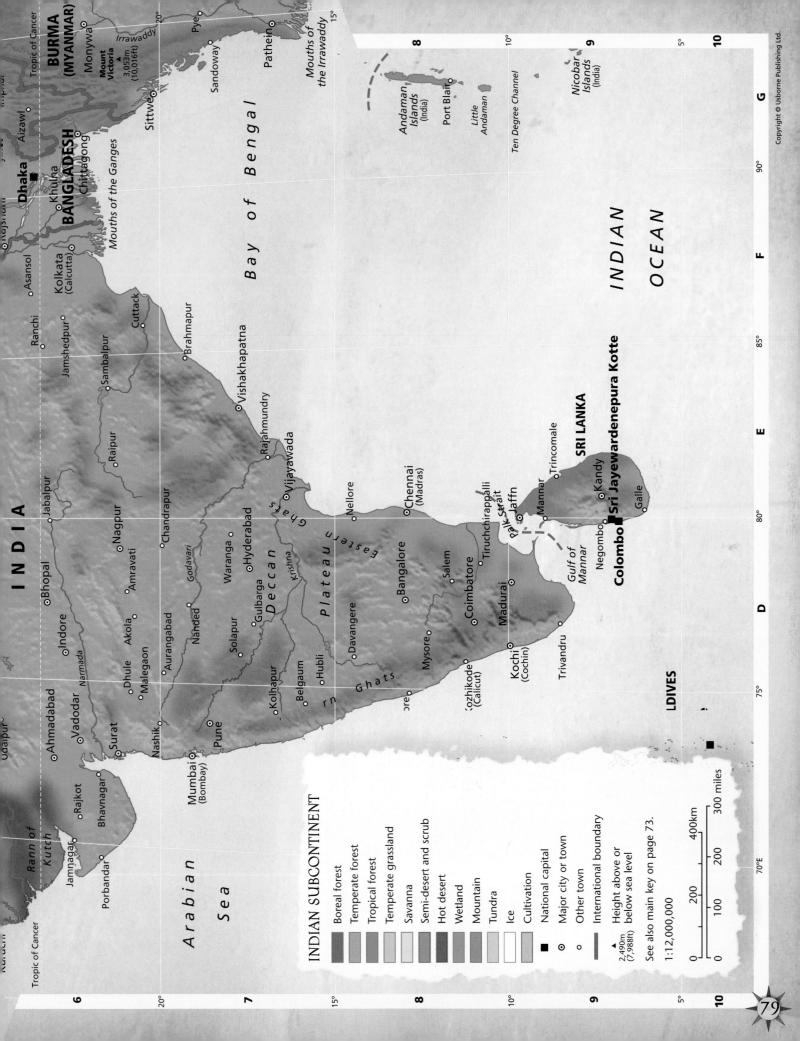

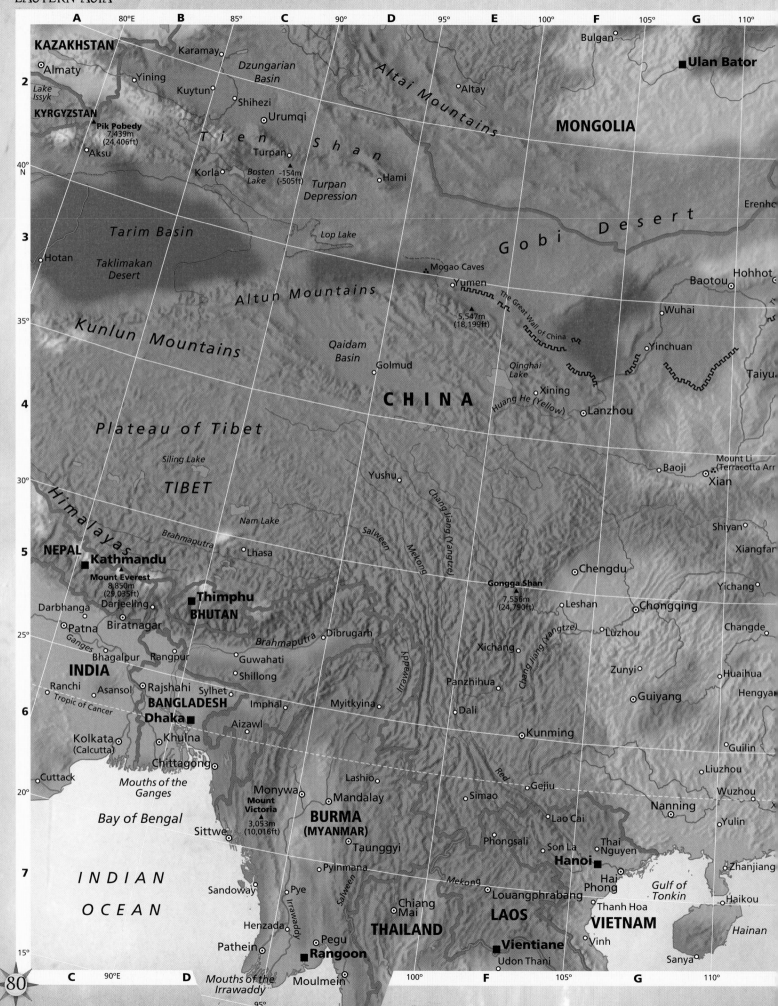

KAZAKHSTAN
Almaty
Lake Issyk
KYRGYZSTAN
Pik Pobedy 7,439m (24,406ft)
Aksu
Yining
Kuytun
Karamay
Dzungarian Basin
Shihezi
Urumqi
Turpan
Korla
Bosten Lake
-154m (-505ft)
Turpan Depression
Hami
Altai Mountains
Altay
Bulgan
Ulan Bator
MONGOLIA
Tien Shan

Hotan
Tarim Basin
Taklimakan Desert
Lop Lake
Altun Mountains
Mogao Caves
Yumen
5,547m (18,199ft)
The Great Wall of China
Gobi Desert
Erenhc
Baotou
Hohhot
Wuhai

Kunlun Mountains
Qaidam Basin
Golmud
Qinghai Lake
Huang He (Yellow)
Xining
Lanzhou
Yinchuan
Taiyu

CHINA

Plateau of Tibet
Siling Lake
TIBET
Nam Lake
Lhasa
Brahmaputra
Yushu
Chang Jiang (Yangtze)
Salween
Mekong
Gongga Shan 7,556m (24,790ft)
Chengdu
Baoji
Xian
Mount Li (Terracotta Arr
Shiyan
Xiangfar
Yichang
Chongqing
Changde

Himalayas
NEPAL
Kathmandu
Mount Everest 8,850m (29,035ft)
Darbhanga
Darjeeling
Thimphu
BHUTAN
Biratnagar
Brahmaputra
Dibrugarh
Guwahati
Shillong
Xichang
Chang Jiang (Yangtze)
Leshan
Luzhou
Zunyi
Guiyang
Huaihua
Hengya

Patna
Ganges
Bhagalpur
Rangpur
INDIA
Ranchi
Asansol
Rajshahi
Sylhet
Imphal
BANGLADESH
Dhaka
Tropic of Cancer
Kolkata (Calcutta)
Khulna
Aizawl
Myitkyina
Panzhihua
Dali
Kunming
Guilin
Liuzhou
Wuzhou

Cuttack
Chittagong
Mouths of the Ganges
Bay of Bengal
Monywa
Mount Victoria 3,053m (10,016ft)
Sittwe
Lashio
Mandalay
BURMA (MYANMAR)
Taunggyi
Simao
Gejiu
Red
Lao Cai
Phongsali
Son La
Thai Nguyen
Hanoi
Hai Phong
Nanning
Yulin
Zhanjiang
Haikou

INDIAN OCEAN
Sandoway
Pye
Henzada
Pathein
Irrawaddy
Salween
Pyinmana
Chiang Mai
THAILAND
Mekong
Louangphrabang
Udon Thani
LAOS
Vientiane
Vinh
VIETNAM
Gulf of Tonkin
Hainan
Sanya

Pegu
Rangoon
Moulmein
Mouths of the Irrawaddy

80

A   90°E   B   95°   C   100°   D   105°   E

Brahmaputra   Lhasa

H i m a l a y a s   *Mekong*   *Chiang jiang (Yangtze)*   Gongga Shan   Chengdu   Wanxian   Enshi

Mount Everest 8,850m (29,035ft)   **Thimphu**   INDIA   7,556m (24,790ft)   Leshan   Chongqing

NEPAL   Darjeeling **BHUTAN**   Xichang   Neijiang   Luzhou   C H

Biratnagar   *Brahmaputra*   Dibrugarh   Zunyi   Huaih

Darbhanga   Rangpur   Jorhat   Zhaotong

Bhagalpur   Guwahati   Panzihua   Guiyang

Asansol   *Ganges*   Shillong   Anshun

25° N   Rajshahi   Sylhet   Dali   Kunming   Liuzhou

Jamshedpur   **BANGLADESH**   Imphal   Myitkyina   Baoshan

Kolkata (Calcutta)   **Dhaka**   Aizawl   *Red*   Kaiyuan   Nannir

Khulna   Lashio   Simao   Gejiu

Chittagong   Monywa   Mandalay   Phongsali   Ha Giang   Qinzhou

Mouths of the Ganges   Mount Victoria 3,053m (10,016ft)   **BURMA (MYANMAR)**   Lao Cai   Thai Nguyen

20°   Sittwe   Meiktila   Taunggyi   Son La   **Hanoi**

Pyinmana   *Salween*   *Mekong*   Louangphrabang   Hai Phong

Bay of Bengal   Pye   Thanh Hoa   *Gulf of Tonkin*

Sandoway   *Irrawaddy*   Chiang Mai   **LAOS**   Vinh

15°   Henzada   Pegu   **Vientiane**   Sanya

Pathein   Thaton   Phitsanulok   Udon Thani   Savannakhet   Hue

Rangoon   Moulmein   Khon Kaen   Da Nang

Mouths of the Irrawaddy   Nakhon Sawan   **THAILAND**   Ubon Ratchathani

I N D I A N   O C E A N   Tavoy   Nakhon Ratchasima   Pakxe   Attapu   **VIETNAM**

Andaman Islands (India)   *Andaman Sea*   **Bangkok**   Stoeng Treng   Qui Nhon

Port Blair   Pattaya   Angkor   *Tonle Sap*   **CAMBODIA**   Buon Me Thuot

Little Andaman   Mergui   Batdambang   Da Lat   Nh. Trar

Mergui Archipelago   Prachuap Khiri Khan   Kampong Chhnang   Kampong Cham

10°   Krong Kaoh Kong   **Phnom Penh**   Bien Hoa

Ten Degree Channel   Chumphon   Kampong Saom   Long Xuyen   *Mekong*   Ho Chi Minh City (Saigon)

Gulf of Thailand   Can Tho

Bac Lieu   *Con Son*

Nicobar Islands (India)   Nakhon Si Thammarat

Hat Yai

Yala

Banda Aceh   Alor Setar   Kota Bharu

5°   Lhokseumawe   George Town (Penang)   Kuala Terengganu

Sumatra   Langsa   Taiping   Ipoh   Gunung Tahan 2,187m (7,175ft)   **MALAYSIA**   *Natuna Islands (Indonesia)*

INDONESIA

A   90°E   B   95°   C   100°   D   105°   E

F 115° 120° G 125°

Yichang
Wuhan
Huangshi
angde
Yueyang
Dongting
Lake
Changsha
Zhuzhou
Hengyang
Chenzhou
Wuzhou
uilin
lin
Zhanjiang
Haikou
Hainan

Hefei
Luan
Nanjing
Wuhu
Nantong
Wuxi
Shanghai
Tai Lake
Hangzhou
Anqing
Ningbo
Poyang
Lake
Nanchang
Linchuan
Wenzhou
Nanping
Yongan
Fuzhou
Ganzhou
Quanzhou
Shaoguan
Zhangzhou
Xiamen
Meizhou
Canton
(Guangzhou)
Xi Jiang
Shantou
Macau
Hong Kong
(Xianggang)

*East
China
Sea*

Ryukyu Island
(Japan)

Chilung
Taipei ■
Taichung
Changhua
TAIWAN
Yu Shan
3,997m
(13,113ft)
Tainan
Kaohsiung

*Sakishima
Islands*

Tropic of Cai

*Batan
Islands*

Luzon Strait

*Babuyan
Islands*

Laoag
Aparri
Tuguegarao
Ilagan
Mount Pulog
2,930m
(9,613ft)
Dagupan
Cabanatuan
Luzon
Olongapo
Quezon City
Manila ■
Lucena
Naga
Calapan
Legaspi
Mindoro
Masbate
Masbate
Roxas
*Calamian
Group*
Panay
Iloilo
Bacolod
Taytay
Cebu
Negros
Surigao
Bohol
Puerto
Princesa
Dumaguete
Butuan
Cagayan de Oro
Palawan
Iligan
Pagadian
Mindanao
Davao
Zamboanga
General Santos

*Philippine
Sea*

PHILIPPINES

P A C I F I C
O C E A N

*South China
Sea*

*Paracel
Islands*

*Spratly
Islands*

Sulu Sea

MALAYSIA
Kota
Kinabalu
Sandakan
Jolo
*Sulu
Archipelago*
**Bandar Seri
Begawan**
BRUNEI
Miri
Tawau
INDONESIA
Bintulu
Borneo
Tarakan

Celebes Sea

*Talaud
Islands*

115° 120° H 125° J 130° K

Copyright © Usborne Publishing Ltd.

MAINLAND SOUTHEAST ASIA

	Boreal forest
	Temperate forest
	Tropical forest
	Temperate grassland
	Savanna
	Semi-desert and scrub
	Hot desert
	Wetland
	Mountain
	Tundra
	Ice
	Cultivation
■	National capital
⊙	Major city or town
○	Other town
	International boundary

▲ 2,490m
(7,988ft)   Height above or
below sea level

See also main key on page 73.

1:12,000,000

0   200   400km
0   100   200   300 miles

15°

5

10°

6

5°

7

A		100°E		B		105°		C		110°		D		115°

MARITIME SOUTHEAST ASIA

Boreal forest	Wetland
Temperate forest	Mountain
Tropical forest	Tundra
Temperate grassland	Ice
Savanna	Cultivation
Semi-desert and scrub	
Hot desert	
International boundary	

■ National capital
⊙ Major city or town
○ Other town

See also main key on page 73.

2,490m
(7,988ft) ▲ Height above or below sea level

1:12,000,000

0   200   400 miles

0   100   200   300 miles

i Nhon

IETNAM

a Trang

South China
Sea

*Spratly
Islands*

Kota
Kinabalu

**Bandar Seri
Begawan
BRUNEI** ■

Miri

Sea
Banda Aceh
Lhokseumawe

Alor Setar

Kota Bharu

Kuala Terengganu

M A L A Y S I A

George Town
(Penang)

Taiping
**Gunung
Tahan**
▲
2,187m
(7,175ft)

Langsa

Ipoh

Kuantan

Bintulu

Medan

*Natuna
Islands*

Sibu

Tarak

Pematangsiantar

*Lake
Toba*

Seremban

Kuala Lumpur ■

*Anambas
Islands*

Simeulue

Melaka

Sumatra

Johor Bahru

Kuching

2,988m
(9,803ft) ▲

Tanjungrede

Sibolga

Strait of Malacca

Singapor
SINGAPORE ■

Pekanbaru

Nias

Pontianak

Riau Islands

Samarinda

Padang

Borneo

Balikpapan

Equator

0°

**Gunung
Kerinci**
▲
3,805m
(12,483ft)

Jambi

Bangka

Pangkalpinang

Karimata Strait

Palangkaraya

*Mentawai
Islands*

Banjarmasin

Palembang

Belitung

Martapura

Bengkulu

Lahat

Baturaja

G r e a t e r   S u n d a   I s l a n d s

I N D O N E S I A

5°
S

Tanjungkarang-
Telukbetung

Java Sea

Krakatoa
▲
813m
(2,667ft)

Serang

Jakarta ■

Bogor

Tegal

Semarang

Lesse

Bandung

Java

Surakarta

Surabaya

Jember

Lombok

Cilacap

Yogyakarta

Malang

Bali

Mataran

Denpasar

Sumbaw

INDIAN

OCEAN

*Christmas
Island
(Australia)*

A		100°E		B		105°		C		110°		D		115°

Country facts and flags

The following pages list the 31 Asian countries that appear in this book, in alphabetical order. There are some key facts about each one, including its area, population (rounded to the nearest 1,000 people), capital city, main and official languages, type of government and the currency used there. Above each entry is the national flag.

AFGHANISTAN

Nationality: Afghan or Afghani
Area: 647,500 sq km
(250,001 sq miles)
Population: 28,717,000
Capital city: Kabul
Main languages: Dari, Pashtu
Government: transitional
Currency: 1 afghani = 100 puls

BANGLADESH

Nationality: Bangladeshi
Area: 144,000 sq km
(55,599 sq miles)
Population: 138,448,000
Capital city: Dhaka
Main languages: Bengali, English
Government: republic
Currency: 1 taka = 100 poisha

BHUTAN

Nationality: Bhutanese
Area: 47,000 sq km
(18,147 sq miles)
Population: 2,140,000
Capital city: Thimphu
Main languages: Dzongkha, Nepali
Government: monarchy
Currency: 1 ngultrum = 100 chetrum

BRUNEI

Nationality: Bruneian
Area: 5,770 sq km (2,228 sq miles)
Population: 358,000
Capital city: Bandar Seri Begawan
Main languages: Malay, English
Government: constitutional sultanate
(a type of monarchy)
Currency: 1 Bruneian dollar = 100 cents

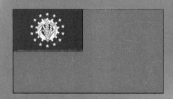

BURMA (MYANMAR)

Nationality: Burmese
Area: 678,500 sq km
(261,970 sq miles)
Population: 42,511,000
Capital city: Rangoon
Main language: Burmese
Government: military dictatorship
Currency: 1 kyat = 100 pyas

CAMBODIA

Nationality: Cambodian
Area: 181,040 sq km
(69,900 sq miles)
Population: 13,125,000
Capital city: Phnom Penh
Main languages: Khmer, French
Government: constitutional monarchy
Currency: 1 new riel = 100 sen

CHINA

Nationality: Chinese
Area: 9,596,960 sq km (3,705,407 sq miles)
Population: 1,295,330,000
Capital city: Beijing
Main languages: Mandarin Chinese, Cantonese, other Chinese dialects
Government: Communist state
Currency: 1 yuan = 10 jiao

EAST TIMOR

Nationality: Timorese
Area: 15,007 sq km (5,794 sq miles)
Population: 998,000
Capital city: Dili
Main languages: Tetum, Portuguese, Indonesian, English
Government: constitutional monarchy
Currency: 1 US dollar = 100 cents

INDIA

Nationality: Indian
Area: 3,287,590 sq km (1,269,346 sq miles)
Population: 1,049,700,000
Capital city: New Delhi
Main languages: Hindi, English, Punjabi, Tamil, over 1,600 other languages and dialects
Government: federal republic
Currency: 1 Indian rupee = 100 paise

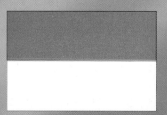

INDONESIA

Nationality: Indonesian
Area: 1,919,440 sq km (741,100 sq miles)
Population: 234,893,000
Capital city: Jakarta
Main languages: Indonesian, English, Javanese
Government: republic
Currency: 1 Indonesian rupiah = 100 sen

JAPAN

Nationality: Japanese
Area: 377,835 sq km (145,883 sq miles)
Population: 127,214,000
Capital city: Tokyo
Main language: Japanese
Government: constitutional monarchy
Currency: 1 yen = 100 sen

KAZAKHSTAN

Nationality: Kazakhstani
Area: 2,717,300 sq km (1,049,155 sq miles)
Population: 16,764,000
Capital city: Astana
Main languages: Kazakh, Russian
Government: republic
Currency: 1 Kazakhstani tenge = 100 tiyn

KYRGYZSTAN

Nationality: Kyrgyzstani
Area: 198,500 sq km (76,641 sq miles)
Population: 4,895,000
Capital city: Bishkek
Main languages: Kyrgyz, Russian
Government: republic
Currency: 1 Krygyzstani som = 100 tyiyn

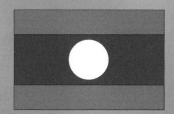

LAOS

Nationality: Lao or Laotian
Area: 236,800 sq km (91,429 sq miles)
Population: 5,922,000
Capital city: Vientiane
Main languages: Lao, French
Government: Communist state
Currency: 1 new kip = 100 at

MALAYSIA

Nationality: Malaysian
Area: 329,750 sq km (127,317 sq miles)
Population: 23,095,000
Capital city: Kuala Lumpur
Main languages: Malay, English, Mandarin Chinese, other Chinese dialects, Tamil
Government: constitutional monarchy
Currency: 1 ringgit = 100 sen

MALDIVES

Nationality: Maldivian
Area: 300 sq km (116 sq miles)
Population: 330,000
Capital city: Male
Main languages: Maldivian, English
Government: republic
Currency: 1 rufiyaa = 100 laari

MONGOLIA

Nationality: Mongolian
Area: 1,565,000 sq km
(604,250 sq miles)
Population: 2,712,000
Capital city: Ulan Bator
Main language: Khalkha Mongol
Government: republic
Currency: 1 tugrik = 100 mongos

NEPAL

Nationality: Nepalese
Area: 140,800 sq km
(54,363 sq miles)
Population: 26,470,000
Capital city: Kathmandu
Main language: Nepali
Government: constitutional monarchy
Currency: 1 Nepalese rupee = 100 paisa

NORTH KOREA

Nationality: Korean
Area: 120,540 sq km
(46,541 sq miles)
Population: 22,446,000
Capital city: Pyongyang
Main language: Korean
Government: authoritarian socialist
Currency: 1 North Korean won = 100 chon

PAKISTAN

Nationality: Pakistani
Area: 803,940 sq km (310,403 sq miles)
Population: 150,695,000
Capital city: Islamabad
Main languages: Punjabi, Sindhi,
Siraiki, Pashtu, Urdu
Government: federal republic
Currency: 1 Pakistani rupee = 100 paisa

PHILIPPINES

Nationality: Philippine
Area: 300,000 sq km
(115,831 sq miles)
Population: 84,620,000
Capital city: Manila
Main languages: Filipino, Tagalog, English
Government: republic
Currency: 1 Philippine peso = 100 centavos

RUSSIA

Nationality: Russian
Area: 17,075,200 sq km
(6,592,772 sq miles)
Population: 144,526,000
Capital city: Moscow
Main language: Russian
Government: federal government
Currency: 1 ruble = 100 kopeks

SINGAPORE

Nationality: Singaporean
Area: 693 sq km (268 sq miles)
Population: 4,609,000
Capital city: Singapore
Main languages: Mandarin Chinese, other
Chinese dialects, Malay, English, Tamil
Government: parliamentary republic
Currency: 1 Singapore dollar = 100 cents

SOUTH KOREA

Nationality: Korean
Area: 98,480 sq km
(38,023 sq miles)
Population: 48,289,000
Capital city: Seoul
Main language: Korean
Government: republic
Currency: 1 South Korean won = 100 chun

SRI LANKA

Nationality: Sri Lankan
Area: 65,610 sq km (25,332 sq miles)
Population: 19,742,000
Capital cities: Colombo/
Sri Jayewardenepura Kotte
Main languages: Sinhala, Tamil, English
Government: republic
Currency: 1 Sri Lankan rupee = 100 cents

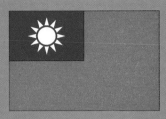

TAIWAN

Nationality: Taiwanese
Area: 35,980 sq km
(13,892 sq miles)
Population: 22,500,000
Capital city: Taipei (Taibei)
Main languages: Taiwanese, Mandarin
Chinese, other Chinese dialects
Government: democracy
Currency: 1 new Taiwan dollar = 100 cents

TAJIKISTAN

Nationality: Tajikistani
Area: 143,100 sq km
(55,251 sq miles)
Population: 6,864,000
Capital city: Dushanbe
Main languages: Tajik, Russian
Government: republic
Currency: 1 Tajikistani somoni
= 100 tanga

THAILAND

Nationality: Thai
Area: 514,000 sq km
(198,457 sq miles)
Population: 64,265,000
Capital city: Bangkok
Main languages: Thai, English
Government: constitutional monarchy
Currency: 1 baht = 100 satang

TURKMENISTAN

Nationality: Turkmen
Area: 488,100 sq km
(188,456 sq miles)
Population: 4,776,000
Capital city: Ashgabat (Ashkhabad)
Main languages: Turkmen, Russian
Government: republic
Currency: 1 Turkmen manat = 100 tenesi

UZBEKISTAN

Nationality: Uzbekistani
Area: 447,400 sq km
(172,742 sq miles)
Population: 25,982,000
Capital city: Tashkent
Main languages: Uzbek, Russian
Government: republic
Currency: 1 Uzbekistani sum = 100 tyyn

VIETNAM

Nationality: Vietnamese
Area: 329,560 sq km (127,244 sq miles)
Population: 81,625,000
Capital city: Hanoi
Main languages: Vietnamese,
French, English
Government: Communist state
Currency: 1 new dong = 100 xu

United Nations

All the Asian countries except for Taiwan (whose independent status is disputed by China) belong to the United Nations. This organization brings countries together to work for peace and development.

ASEAN

Ten countries in southeastern Asia – Laos, Burma (Myanmar), Cambodia, Indonesia, Brunei, Philippines, Malaysia, Thailand, Singapore and Vietnam – belong to the Association of Southeast Asian Nations (ASEAN). They work together for economic growth, cultural development, and to promote peace between the countries in the region.

The ASEAN flag features a bundle of ten rice stalks, which represents the member countries bound together in friendship.

INTERNET LINKS

For a link to a website where you can find out more about cultures and religions in many Asian countries, go to **www.usborne-quicklinks.com**

Map index

This is an index of the places and features named on the maps on pages 74–85. Each entry is made up of the following parts: the name (in **bold** type), the country or region within which it is located (in *italics*), the page on which the name can be found (in **bold** type) and the grid reference (also in **bold** type). For some names, there is also a description explaining what kind of place it is, for example a country or national capital. To find a place on a map, first find the map indicated by the page reference, then use the grid to find the square containing the name.

Colombo, *Sri Lanka, national capital*, 79 D9
Communism Peak, *Tajikistan*, 78 C3
Con Son, *Vietnam*, 82 E6
Constanta, *Romania*, 76 A3
Corum, *Turkey*, 76 B3
Cuttack, *India*, 79 F6, 80 C6
Cyprus, *Europe/Asia, country*, 76 B4
Czech Republic, *Europe, country*, 74 A3

D

Dagupan, *Philippines*, 83 H4
Dahlak Archipelago, *Eritrea*, 77 D8
Da Lat, *Vietnam*, 82 E5
Dali, *China*, 80 F5, 82 D2
Dalian, *China*, 81 K3
Damascus, *Syria, national capital*, 76 C5
Damavand, *Iran*, 74 C4, 76 F4
Da Nang, *Vietnam*, 82 E4
Dandong, *China*, 81 K2
Daqing, *China*, 81 L1
Darbhanga, *India*, 78 F5, 80 C5, 82 A2
Darjeeling, *India*, 78 F5, 80 C5, 82 A2
Darwin, *Australia*, 85 H6
Dasht-e Kavir, *Iran*, 76 F5
Dasoguz, *Turkmenistan*, 74 C3, 76 G3
Datong, *China*, 81 H2
Davangere, *India*, 79 D8
Davao, *Philippines*, 83 J6, 85 G2
Dayr az Zawr, *Syria*, 76 D4
Deccan Plateau, *India*, 79 D7
Delhi, *India*, 78 D5
Denizli, *Turkey*, 76 A4
Denmark, *Europe, country*, 74 A3
Denpasar, *Indonesia*, 84 E5
D'Entrecasteaux Islands, *Papua New Guinea*, 85 M5
Dera Ghazi Khan, *Pakistan*, 78 C4
Derbent, *Russia*, 76 E3
Dese, *Ethiopia*, 77 C9
Dhaka, *Bangladesh, national capital*, 79 G6, 80 C6
Dhamar, *Yemen*, 77 D9
Dhule, *India*, 79 C6
Dibrugarh, *India*, 78 G5, 80 D5, 82 D2
Dikhil, *Djibouti*, 77 D9
Dili, *East Timor, national capital*, 85 G5
Dire Dawa, *Ethiopia*, 77 D9
Diyarbakir, *Turkey*, 76 D4
Djibouti, *Africa, country*, 77 D9
Djibouti, *Djibouti, national capital*, 77 D9
Doha, *Qatar, national capital*, 74 D4, 77 F6
Dolak, *Indonesia*, 85 J5
Dongting Lake, *China*, 81 H5, 83 F2
Dnipropetrovsk, *Ukraine*, 74 B3
Dubai, *United Arab Emirates*, 77 G6
Dumaguete, *Philippines*, 83 H6, 85 F2
Dushanbe, *Tajikistan, national capital*, 74 D4, 78 B3
Dzungarian Basin, *China*, 78 F1, 80 C1

E

East China Sea, *Asia*, 81 K5, 83 H2
Eastern Ghats, *India*, 79 D8
East Siberian Sea, *Russia*, 75 J2
East Timor, *Asia, country*, 85 G5
Egypt, *Africa, country*, 77 B7
Elat, *Israel*, 77 B6
Elazig, *Turkey*, 76 C4
Elbrus, Mount, *Russia*, 74 C3, 76 D3
Elista, *Russia*, 76 D2
El Mansura, *Egypt*, 77 B5
El Minya, *Egypt*, 77 B6
Embi, *Kazakhstan*, 76 G2
Empty Quarter, *Asia*, 77 E8
Ende, *Indonesia*, 85 F5
Enshi, *China*, 82 E1
Erenhot, *China*, 80 H2
Eritrea, *Africa, country*, 77 C8
Erzurum, *Turkey*, 76 D4
Esfahan, *Iran*, 74 C4, 76 F5
Eskisehir, *Turkey*, 76 B3
Estonia, *Europe, country*, 74 B3
Ethiopia, *Africa, country*, 77 C9
Ethiopian Highlands, *Ethiopia*, 77 C9
Euphrates, *Asia*, 77 E5
Everest, Mount, *Asia*, 78 F5, 80 C5, 82 A2

F

Faisalabad, *Pakistan*, 78 C4
Fakfak, *Indonesia*, 85 H4
Farasan Islands, *Saudi Arabia*, 77 D8
Fargona, *Uzbekistan*, 78 C2
Finland, *Europe, country*, 74 B2
Flores, *Indonesia*, 85 F5
Flores Sea, *Indonesia*, 85 F5
France, *Europe, country*, 74 A3
Franz Josef Land, *Russia*, 74 C1
Fuji, Mount, *Japan*, 81 N3
Fukui, *Japan*, 81 N3
Fukuoka, *Japan*, 81 M4
Fukushima, *Japan*, 81 P3
Fushun, *China*, 81 K2
Fuxin, *China*, 81 K2
Fuzhou, *China*, 81 J5, 83 G2

G

Galle, *Sri Lanka*, 79 E9
Ganca, *Azerbaijan*, 76 E3
Ganges, *Asia*, 78 E5, 80 C5, 82 A3
Ganges, Mouths of the, *Asia*, 79 F6, 80 C6, 82 A3
Ganzhou, *China*, 81 H5, 83 F2
Gaza, *Israel*, 77 B5
Gaziantep, *Turkey*, 76 C4
Gedaref, *Sudan*, 77 C9
Gejiu, *China*, 80 F6, 82 D3
General Santos, *Philippines*, 83 J6, 85 G2
George Town, *Malaysia*, 82 D6, 84 B2
Georgia, *Asia, country*, 74 C3, 76 D3
Germany, *Europe, country*, 74 A3
Gilgit, *Pakistan*, 78 C3
Giza, Pyramids of, *Egypt*, 77 B6
Gobi Desert, *Asia*, 75 F3, 80 F2
Godavari, *India*, 79 D7
Golmud, *China*, 78 G3, 80 D3
Gonder, *Ethiopia*, 77 C9
Gongga Shan, *China*, 80 F5, 82 D2
Gorakhpur, *India*, 78 E5
Gorgan, *Iran*, 76 F4
Gori, *Georgia*, 76 D3
Gorontalo, *Indonesia*, 85 F3
Grand Canal, *China*, 81 J4
Greater Khingan Range, *China*, 81 J1
Greater Sunda Islands, *Asia*, 84 C4
Great Salt Desert, *Iran*, 76 F5
Great Wall of China, *China*, 75 E4, 80 F3, 81 H2
Groznyy, *Russia*, 76 E3
Guangzhou, *China*, 81 H6, 83 F3
Guilin, *China*, 80 H5, 83 F2
Guiyang, *China*, 80 G5, 82 E2
Gujranwala, *Pakistan*, 78 C4
Gujrat, *Pakistan*, 78 C4
Gulbarga, *India*, 79 D7
Gulf, The, *Asia*, 77 F6
Gunung Kerinci, *Indonesia*, 84 B4
Gunung Tahan, *Malaysia*, 82 D7, 84 B3
Guwahati, *India*, 78 G5, 80 D5, 82 B2
Gwalior, *India*, 78 D5

H

Hadhramaut, *Yemen*, 77 E9
Hagen, Mount, *Papua New Guinea*, 85 K5
Ha Giang, *Vietnam*, 82 E3
Haifa, *Israel*, 76 B5
Haikou, *China*, 80 H6, 83 F3
Hail, *Saudi Arabia*, 77 D6
Hailar, *China*, 81 J1
Hainan, *China*, 80 H7, 83 F4
Hai Phong, *Vietnam*, 80 G6, 82 E3
Hakodate, *Japan*, 75 H3, 81 P2
Halmahera, *Indonesia*, 85 G3
Hamadan, *Iran*, 76 E5
Hamah, *Syria*, 76 C4
Hamamatsu, *Japan*, 81 N4
Hamhung, *North Korea*, 81 L3
Hami, *China*, 78 G2, 80 D2
Handan, *China*, 81 H3
Hangzhou, *China*, 81 K4, 83 H1
Hanoi, *Vietnam, national capital*, 80 G6, 82 E3
Haradh, *Saudi Arabia*, 77 E7
Harbin, *China*, 81 L1
Hargeysa, *Ethiopia*, 77 D9

Hat Yai, *Thailand*, 82 D6, 84 B2
Hefei, *China*, 81 J4, 83 G1
Hegang, *China*, 81 M1
Hejaz, *Saudi Arabia*, 77 C6
Helmand, *Asia*, 77 H5, 78 B4
Hengyang, *China*, 80 H5, 83 F2
Henzada, *Burma*, 80 E7, 82 C4
Herat, *Afghanistan*, 74 D4, 76 H5, 78 A4
Himalayas, *Asia*, 78 E4, 80 B5, 82 A2
Hindu Kush, *Asia*, 78 B3
Hiroshima, *Japan*, 81 M4
Ho Chi Minh City, *Vietnam*, 82 E5
Hohhot, *China*, 80 H2
Hokkaido, *Japan*, 75 H3, 81 P2
Homs, *Syria*, 76 C5
Hong Kong, *China*, 81 H6, 83 F3
Honshu, *Japan*, 75 H4, 81 N3
Hormuz, Strait of, *Asia*, 77 G6
Hotan, *China*, 74 D4, 78 D3, 80 A3
Huaihua, *China*, 80 G5, 82 E2
Huang He, *China*, 75 F4, 80 F3, 81 H3
Huangshi, *China*, 83 G1
Hubli, *India*, 79 D7
Hue, *Vietnam*, 82 E4
Hulun Lake, *China*, 81 J1
Hungary, *Europe, country*, 74 A3
Hurghada, *Egypt*, 77 B6
Hyderabad, *India*, 79 D7
Hyderabad, *Pakistan*, 78 B5
Hyesan, *North Korea*, 81 L2

I

Ibb, *Yemen*, 77 D9
Ilagan, *Philippines*, 83 H4
Iligan, *Philippines*, 83 H6, 85 F2
Iloilo, *Philippines*, 83 H5, 85 F1
Imphal, *India*, 79 G6, 80 D6, 82 B3
Inchon, *South Korea*, 81 L3
Inderbor, *Kazakhstan*, 76 F2
India, *Asia, country*, 74 D4, 79 D6, 80 C6, 82 B2
Indian Ocean, 77, 79, 80, 82, 84
Indonesia, *Asia, country*, 82 C7, 84 C5
Indore, *India*, 79 D6
Indus, *Asia*, 74 D4, 78 B5
Inner Mongolia, *China*, 81 H2
Ipoh, *Malaysia*, 82 D7, 84 B3
Iran, *Asia, country*, 76 F5
Iranshahr, *Iran*, 77 H6
Iraq, *Asia, country*, 74 C4, 76 D5
Irbid, *Jordan*, 76 C5
Irkutsk, *Russia*, 75 F3
Irrawaddy, *Burma*, 79 G6, 80 E5, 82 C4
Irrawaddy, Mouths of the, *Burma*, 79 G7, 80 D7, 82 B4
Irtysh, *Russia*, 74 D2
Islamabad, *Pakistan, national capital*, 74 D4, 78 C4
Ismailia, *Egypt*, 77 B5
Isparta, *Turkey*, 76 B4
Israel, *Asia, country*, 77 B5
Issyk, Lake, *Kyrgyzstan*, 78 D2, 80 A2
Istanbul, *Turkey*, 76 A3

J

Jabalpur, *India*, 79 D6
Jaffna, *Sri Lanka*, 79 E9
Jaipur, *India*, 78 D5
Jakarta, *Indonesia, national capital*, 84 C5
Jalalabad, *Afghanistan*, 78 C4
Jalal-Abad, *Kyrgyzstan*, 78 C2
Jambi, *Indonesia*, 84 B4
Jammu, *India*, 78 C4
Jammu and Kashmir, *Asia*, 78 D4
Jamnagar, *India*, 79 C6
Jamshedpur, *India*, 79 F6, 82 A3
Japan, *Asia, country*, 75 H4, 81 N3
Japan, Sea of, *Asia*, 75 G3, 81 M2
Java, *Indonesia*, 84 C5
Java Sea, *Indonesia*, 84 C5
Jayapura, *Indonesia*, 85 K4
Jedda, *Saudi Arabia*, 77 C7
Jember, *Indonesia*, 84 D5
Jerusalem, *Israel, national capital*, 77 C5
Jhansi, *India*, 78 D5
Jiamusi, *China*, 75 G3, 81 M1

Jilin, *China*, 81 L2
Jinhua, *China*, 81 J5, 83 G2
Jining, *China*, 81 J3
Jinzhou, *China*, 81 K2
Jixi, *China*, 81 M1
Jizzax, *Uzbekistan*, 78 B2
Jodhpur, *India*, 78 C5
Johor Bahru, *Malaysia*, 84 B3
Jolo, *Philippines*, 83 H6, 85 F2
Jordan, *Asia, country*, 77 C5
Jorhat, *India*, 78 G5, 82 B2

K

K2, *Asia*, 74 D4, 78 D3
Kabul, *Afghanistan, national capital*, 74 D4, 78 B4
Kagoshima, *Japan*, 81 M4
Kahramanmaras, *Turkey*, 76 C4
Kaiyuan, *China*, 82 D3
Kamchatka Peninsula, *Russia*, 75 H3
Kampong Cham, *Cambodia*, 82 E5
Kampong Chhnang, *Cambodia*, 82 D5
Kampong Saom, *Cambodia*, 82 D5
Kanazawa, *Japan*, 81 N3
Kandahar, *Afghanistan*, 74 D4, 78 B4
Kandy, *Sri Lanka*, 79 E9
Kanggye, *North Korea*, 81 L2
Kanpur, *India*, 78 E5
Kaohsiung, *Taiwan*, 81 K6, 83 H3
Kara-Balta, *Kyrgyzstan*, 78 C2
Karabuk, *Turkey*, 76 B3
Karachi, *Pakistan*, 79 B6
Karaj, *Iran*, 76 F4
Karakol, *Kyrgyzstan*, 78 D2
Karakorum Range, *Asia*, 78 D3
Kara Kum Desert, *Turkmenistan*, 76 G3
Karamay, *China*, 78 E1, 80 B1
Kara Sea, *Russia*, 74 D2
Karimata Strait, *Indonesia*, 84 C4
Karora, *Eritrea*, 77 C8
Kashi, *China*, 78 D3
Kassala, *Sudan*, 77 C8
Kathmandu, *Nepal, national capital*, 78 F5, 80 C5
Kayseri, *Turkey*, 76 C4
Kazakhstan, *Asia, country*, 74 C3, 76 G2, 78 B1, 80 A2
Kazan, *Russia*, 74 C3
Kendari, *Indonesia*, 85 F4
Kerch, *Ukraine*, 76 C2
Kerema, *Papua New Guinea*, 85 L5
Keren, *Eritrea*, 77 C8
Kerman, *Iran*, 77 G5
Kermanshah, *Iran*, 76 E5
Khabarovsk, *Russia*, 75 G3
Khanka, Lake, *Asia*, 81 M2
Kharkiv, *Ukraine*, 74 B3
Kherson, *Ukraine*, 76 B2
Khon Kaen, *Thailand*, 82 D4
Khorugh, *Tajikistan*, 78 C3
Khujand, *Tajikistan*, 78 B2
Khulna, *Bangladesh*, 79 F6, 80 C6, 82 A3
Kiev, *Ukraine, national capital*, 74 B3
Kimchaek, *North Korea*, 81 L2
Kings, Valley of the, *Egypt*, 77 B6
Kirkuk, *Iraq*, 76 D4
Kitakyushu, *Japan*, 81 M4
Kobar Sink, *Ethiopia*, 77 D9
Kochi, *India*, 79 D9
Kokshetau, *Kazakhstan*, 76 J1
Kola Peninsula, *Russia*, 74 B2
Kolhapur, *India*, 79 C7
Kolkata, *India*, 79 F6, 80 C6, 82 A3
Kolmya Range, *Russia*, 75 H2
Komsomolsk, *Russia*, 75 G3
Konduz, *Afghanistan*, 78 B3
Kongur Shan, *China*, 78 D3
Konya, *Turkey*, 76 B4
Korea Bay, *Asia*, 81 K3
Korea Strait, *Asia*, 81 L4
Korla, *China*, 78 F2, 80 C2
Kota, *India*, 78 D5
Kota Bharu, *Malaysia*, 82 D6, 84 B2
Kota Kinabalu, *Malaysia*, 83 G6, 84 E2
Kozhikode, *India*, 79 D8
Krakatoa, *Indonesia*, 84 C5

Krasnodar, *Russia*, 74 C3, 76 C2
Krasnoyarsk, *Russia*, 74 E3
Krishna, *India*, 79 D7
Krong Kaoh Kong, *Cambodia*, 82 D5
Kuala Lumpur, *Malaysia, national capital*, 84 B3
Kuala Terengganu, *Malaysia*, 82 D6, 84 B2
Kuantan, *Malaysia*, 84 B3
Kuching, *Malaysia*, 84 D3
Kulob, *Tajikistan*, 78 B3
Kumamoto, *Japan*, 81 M4
Kunlun Mountains, *China*, 78 E3, 80 B3
Kunming, *China*, 80 F5, 82 D2
Kupang, *Indonesia*, 85 F6
Kuril Islands, *Russia*, 75 H3, 81 Q2
Kushiro, *Japan*, 81 P2
Kutahya, *Turkey*, 76 A4
Kutaisi, *Georgia*, 76 D3
Kutch, Rann of, *India*, 79 B6
Kuwait, *Asia, country*, 74 C4, 77 E6
Kuwait City, *Kuwait, national capital*, 74 C4, 77 E6
Kuytun, *China*, 78 F2, 80 B2
Kwangju, *South Korea*, 81 L3
Kyoto, *Japan*, 81 N3
Kyrgyzstan, *Asia, country*, 74 D3, 78 C2, 80 A2
Kyushu, *Japan*, 81 M4
Kyzyl, *Russia*, 74 E3

L

Ladoga, Lake, *Russia*, 74 B2
Lae, *Papua New Guinea*, 85 L5
Lahat, *Indonesia*, 84 B4
Lahore, *Pakistan*, 74 D4, 78 C4
Langsa, *Indonesia*, 82 C7, 84 A3
Lanzhou, *China*, 75 F4, 80 F3
Laoag, *Philippines*, 81 K7, 83 H4
Lao Cai, *Vietnam*, 80 F6, 82 D3
Laos, *Asia, country*, 80 F7, 82 D4
La Perouse Strait, *Asia*, 81 P1
Laptev Sea, *Russia*, 75 G2
Larkana, *Pakistan*, 78 B5
Lashio, *Burma*, 80 E6, 82 C3
Latakia, *Syria*, 76 C4
Latvia, *Europe, country*, 74 B3
Lebanon, *Asia, country*, 76 C5
Legaspi, *Philippines*, 83 H5, 85 F1
Lena, *Russia*, 75 G2
Leshan, *China*, 80 F5, 82 D2
Lesser Sunda Islands, *Indonesia*, 84 E5
Lhasa, *China*, 78 G5, 80 D5, 82 B2
Lhokseumawe, *Indonesia*, 82 C6, 84 A2
Li, Mount, *China*, 80 G4
Lianyungang, *China*, 81 J4
Liaoyuan, *China*, 81 L2
Limassol, *Cyprus*, 76 B5
Linchuan, *China*, 81 J5, 83 G2
Lithuania, *Europe, country*, 74 B3
Little Andaman, *India*, 79 G8, 82 B5
Liuzhou, *China*, 80 G6, 82 E3
Lombok, *Indonesia*, 84 E5
London, *UK, national capital*, 74 A3
Long Xuyen, *Vietnam*, 82 E5
Lop Lake, *China*, 78 G2, 80 D2
Louangphrabang, *Laos*, 80 F7, 82 D4
Luan, *China*, 83 G1
Lucena, *Philippines*, 83 H5, 85 F1
Lucknow, *India*, 78 E5
Ludhiana, *India*, 78 D4
Luxembourg, *Europe, country*, 74 A3
Luxor, *Egypt*, 77 B6
Luzhou, *China*, 80 G5, 82 E2
Luzon, *Philippines*, 81 K7, 83 H4
Luzon Strait, *Philippines*, 81 K7, 83 H4
Lviv, *Ukraine*, 74 B3

M

Maan, *Jordan*, 77 C5
Macau, *China*, 81 H6, 83 F3
Madang, *Papua New Guinea*, 85 L5
Madras, *India*, 79 E8
Madurai, *India*, 79 D9
Magadan, *Russia*, 75 H3
Magnitogorsk, *Russia*, 76 G1
Makassar Strait, *Indonesia*, 85 E4
Makhachkala, *Russia*, 76 E3
Malacca, Strait of, *Asia*, 84 B3

Malang, *Indonesia*, 84 D5
Malatya, *Turkey*, 76 C4
Malaysia, *Asia, country*, 82 D7, 84 B2
Maldives, *Asia, country*, 79 C9
Male, *Maldives, national capital*, 79 C10
Malegaon, *India*, 79 C6
Manado, *Indonesia*, 85 F3
Manama, *Bahrain, national capital*, 74 C4, 77 F6
Manchuria, *China*, 81 K2
Mandalay, *Burma*, 80 E6, 82 C3
Mangalore, *India*, 79 C8
Manila, *Philippines, national capital*, 83 H5, 85 F1
Mannar, *Sri Lanka*, 79 E9
Mannar, Gulf of, *Asia*, 79 D9
Manzhouli, *China*, 75 F3
Maoke Range, *Indonesia*, 85 J4
Marib, *Yemen*, 77 E8
Mariupol, *Ukraine*, 76 C2
Martapura, *Indonesia*, 84 D4
Mary, *Turkmenistan*, 76 H4, 78 A3
Masbate, *Philippines*, 83 H5, 85 F1
Mashhad, *Iran*, 74 C4, 76 G4
Masirah Island, *Oman*, 77 G7
Massawa, *Eritrea*, 77 C8
Mataram, *Indonesia*, 84 E5
Matsuyama, *Japan*, 81 M4
Mazar-e Sharif, *Afghanistan*, 74 D4, 78 B3
Mecca, *Saudi Arabia*, 77 C7
Medan, *Indonesia*, 84 A3
Medina, *Saudi Arabia*, 77 C7
Mediterranean Sea, *Europe/Africa*, 76 B5
Meerut, *India*, 78 D5
Meiktila, *Burma*, 82 C3
Meizhou, *China*, 81 J6, 83 G3
Mekele, *Ethiopia*, 77 C9
Mekong, *Asia*, 80 E4, 82 E5
Melaka, *Malaysia*, 84 B3
Mentawai Islands, *Indonesia*, 84 A4
Mergui, *Burma*, 82 C5
Mergui Archipelago, *Burma*, 82 C5
Mersin, *Turkey*, 76 B4
Minsk, *Belarus, national capital*, 74 B3
Miri, *Malaysia*, 83 F7, 84 D3
Misool, *Indonesia*, 85 H4
Mogao Caves, *China*, 78 H2, 80 E2
Moldova, *Europe, country*, 74 B3, 76 A2
Molucca Sea, *Indonesia*, 85 F4
Mongolia, *Asia, country*, 75 F3, 78 H1, 80 F1
Monywa, *Burma*, 79 H6, 80 E6, 82 C3
Morotai, *Indonesia*, 85 G3
Moscow, *Russia, national capital*, 74 B3
Mosul, *Iraq*, 74 C4, 76 D4
Moulmein, *Burma*, 80 E7, 82 C4
Mount Hagen, *Papua New Guinea*, 85 K5
Mount Li, *China*, 80 G4
Mudanjiang, *China*, 81 L2
Multan, *Pakistan*, 78 C4
Mumbai, *India*, 79 C7
Murmansk, *Russia*, 74 B2
Muscat, *Oman, national capital*, 77 G7
Myanmar, *Asia, country*, 79 G6, 80 E6, 82 C3
Myitkyina, *Burma*, 80 E5, 82 C2
Mykolayiv, *Ukraine*, 76 B2
Mysore, *India*, 79 D8

N

Naga, *Philippines*, 83 H5, 85 F1
Nagasaki, *Japan*, 81 L4
Nagoya, *Japan*, 81 N3
Nagpur, *India*, 79 D6
Najran, *Saudi Arabia*, 77 D8
Nakhodka, *Russia*, 81 M2
Nakhon Ratchasima, *Thailand*, 82 D5
Nakhon Sawan, *Thailand*, 82 D4
Nakhon Si Thammarat, *Thailand*, 82 D6
Nalchik, *Russia*, 76 D3
Namangan, *Uzbekistan*, 78 C2
Nam Lake, *China*, 78 G4, 80 D3
Nampo, *North Korea*, 81 L3
Nanchang, *China*, 81 J5, 83 G2
Nanded, *India*, 79 D7
Nanjing, *China*, 81 J4, 83 G1

Nanning, *China*, 80 G6, 82 E3
Nanping, *China*, 81 J5, 83 G2
Nantong, *China*, 83 H1
Narmada, *India*, 79 C6
Nashik, *India*, 79 C6
Nasser, Lake, *Egypt*, 77 B7
Natuna Islands, *Indonesia*, 82 E7, 84 C3
Navoiy, *Uzbekistan*, 76 J3, 78 B2
Nawabshah, *Pakistan*, 78 B5
Naxcivan, *Azerbaijan*, 76 E4
Negombo, *Sri Lanka*, 79 D9
Negros, *Philippines*, 83 H6, 85 F2
Neijiang, *China*, 82 E2
Nellore, *India*, 79 E8
Nepal, *Asia, country*, 78 E5, 80 B5, 82 A2
Netherlands, *Europe, country*, 74 A3
New Britain, *Papua New Guinea*, 85 M5
New Delhi, *India, national capital*, 78 D5
New Guinea, *Asia/Oceania*, 85 J4
New Ireland, *Papua New Guinea*, 85 M4
New Siberia Islands, *Russia*, 75 H2
Nha Trang, *Vietnam*, 82 E5, 84 C1
Nias, *Indonesia*, 84 A3
Nicobar Islands, *India*, 79 G9, 82 B6
Nicosia, *Cyprus, national capital*, 76 B4
Niigata, *Japan*, 81 N3
Nile, *Africa*, 77 B6
Nile Delta, *Africa*, 77 B5
Ningbo, *China*, 81 K5, 83 H2
Nizhniy Novgorod, *Russia*, 74 C3
Norilsk, *Russia*, 74 E2
North Cape, *Norway*, 74 B2
Northern Territory, *Australia*, 85 H6
North Korea, *Asia, country*, 81 L2
North Sea, *Europe*, 74 A2
Norway, *Europe, country*, 74 A2
Norwegian Sea, *Europe*, 74 A2
Novaya Zemlya, *Russia*, 74 C2
Novorossiysk, *Russia*, 76 C3
Novosibirsk, *Russia*, 74 E3
Novyy Urengoy, *Russia*, 74 D2
Nubian Desert, *Africa*, 77 B7
Nukus, *Uzbekistan*, 74 C3, 76 G3

O

Ob, *Russia*, 74 D2
Obi, *Indonesia*, 85 G4
Odesa, *Ukraine*, 74 B3, 76 B2
Okayama, *Japan*, 81 M4
Okhotsk, Sea of, *Asia*, 75 H3
Okinawa, *Japan*, 81 L5
Olongapo, *Philippines*, 83 H5, 85 F1
Oman, *Asia, country*, 77 G6
Oman, Gulf of, *Asia*, 77 G7
Omsk, *Russia*, 74 D3
Onega, Lake, *Russia*, 74 B2
Oral, *Kazakhstan*, 74 C3, 76 F1
Orenburg, *Russia*, 74 C3, 76 G1
Orsk, *Russia*, 76 G1
Osaka, *Japan*, 81 N4
Osh, *Kyrgyzstan*, 74 D3, 78 C2
Oslo, *Norway, national capital*, 74 A3

P

Pacific Ocean, 75, 81, 83, 85
Padang, *Indonesia*, 84 B4
Pagadian, *Philippines*, 83 H6, 85 F2
Pakistan, *Asia, country*, 74 D4, 77 H6, 78 B5
Pakxe, *Laos*, 82 E4
Palangkaraya, *Indonesia*, 84 D4
Palau, *Oceania, country*, 85 J3
Palawan, *Philippines*, 83 G6, 85 E2
Palembang, *Indonesia*, 84 B4
Palk Strait, *Asia*, 79 D9
Palopo, *Indonesia*, 85 F4
Palu, *Indonesia*, 85 E4
Panay, *Philippines*, 83 H5, 85 F1
Pangkalpinang, *Indonesia*, 84 C4
Panjgur, *Pakistan*, 77 H6, 78 A5
Panzhihua, *China*, 80 F5, 82 D2
Papua, Gulf of, *Papua New Guinea*, 85 K5
Papua New Guinea, *Oceania, country*, 85 L5
Paracel Islands, *Asia*, 83 F4
Parepare, *Indonesia*, 85 E4
Paris, *France, national capital*, 74 A3
Pathein, *Burma*, 79 G7, 80 D7, 82 B4

Patna, *India*, 78 F5, 80 C5
Pattaya, *Thailand*, 82 D5
Pavlodar, *Kazakhstan*, 74 D3
Pegu, *Burma*, 80 E7, 82 C4
Pekanbaru, *Indonesia*, 84 B3
Peleng, *Indonesia*, 85 F4
Pematangsiantar, *Indonesia*, 84 A3
Penang, *Malaysia*, 82 D6, 84 B2
Perm, *Russia*, 74 C3
Persepolis, *Iran*, 77 F6
Persian Gulf, *Asia*, 74 C4, 77 F6
Peshawar, *Pakistan*, 78 C4
Petra, *Jordan*, 77 C5
Petropavlovsk-Kamchatskiy, *Russia*, 75 H3
Philippines, *Asia, country*, 81 K7, 83 J5, 85 G1
Philippine Sea, *Asia*, 83 H5, 85 G1
Phitsanulok, *Thailand*, 82 D4
Phnom Penh, *Cambodia, national capital*, 82 D5
Phongsali, *Laos*, 80 F6, 82 D3
Pik Pobedy, *Asia*, 78 E2, 80 B2
Pingdingshan, *China*, 81 H4
Pokhara, *Nepal*, 78 E5
Poland, *Europe, country*, 74 A3
Pontianak, *Indonesia*, 84 C3
Porbandar, *India*, 79 B6
Port Blair, *India*, 79 G8, 82 B5
Port Moresby, *Papua New Guinea, national capital*, 85 L5
Port Said, *Egypt*, 77 B5
Port Sudan, *Sudan*, 77 C8
Poti, *Georgia*, 76 D3
Poyang Lake, *China*, 81 J5, 83 G2
Prachuap Khiri Khan, *Thailand*, 82 C5
Puerto Princesa, *Philippines*, 83 G6, 85 E2
Pulog, Mount, *Philippines*, 83 H4
Puncak Jaya, *Indonesia*, 85 J4
Pune, *India*, 79 C7
Pusan, *South Korea*, 81 L3
Pye, *Burma*, 79 H7, 80 E7, 82 C4
Pyinmana, *Burma*, 80 E7, 82 C4
Pyongyang, *North Korea, national capital*, 81 L3

Q

Qaidam Basin, *China*, 78 G3, 80 D3
Qaraghandy, *Kazakhstan*, 74 D3
Qatar, *Asia, country*, 74 C4, 77 F6
Qazvin, *Iran*, 76 E4
Qena, *Egypt*, 77 B6
Qingdao, *China*, 81 K3
Qinghai Lake, *China*, 75 F4, 80 F3
Qinhuangdao, *China*, 81 J3
Qinzhou, *China*, 82 E3
Qiqihar, *China*, 81 K1
Qom, *Iran*, 76 F5
Qostanay, *Kazakhstan*, 76 H1
Quanzhou, *China*, 81 J6, 83 G3
Quetta, *Pakistan*, 78 B4
Quezon City, *Philippines*, 83 H5, 85 F1
Qui Nhon, *Vietnam*, 82 E5, 84 C1
Qurghonteppa, *Tajikistan*, 78 B3
Quzhou, *China*, 83 G2
Qyzylorda, *Kazakhstan*, 74 D3, 76 J3, 78 B2

R

Rabaul, *Papua New Guinea*, 85 M4
Rahimyar Khan, *Pakistan*, 78 C5
Raipur, *India*, 79 E6
Rajahmundry, *India*, 79 E7
Rajkot, *India*, 79 C6
Rajshahi, *Bangladesh*, 79 F6, 80 C6, 82 A3
Ranchi, *India*, 79 F6, 80 C6
Rangoon, *Burma, national capital*, 80 E7, 82 C4
Rangpur, *Bangladesh*, 78 F5, 80 C5, 82 A2
Ras Dashen, *Ethiopia*, 77 C9
Rasht, *Iran*, 76 E4
Red, *Asia, river*, 80 F6, 82 D3
Red Sea, *Africa/Asia*, 77 C7
Riau Islands, *Indonesia*, 84 B3
Riyadh, *Saudi Arabia, national capital*, 74 C4, 77 E7
Romania, *Europe, country*, 74 B3
Rostov, *Russia*, 74 B3, 76 C2
Roti, *Indonesia*, 85 F6
Roxas, *Philippines*, 83 H5, 85 F1
Rub al Khali, *Asia*, 77 E8
Rudnyy, *Kazakhstan*, 76 H1

Russia, *Asia/Europe, country,* 74 E3, 76 D2, 81 M1
Ryazan, *Russia,* 74 B3
Ryukyu Islands, *Japan,* 81 L5, 83 H2

S

Sabzevar, *Iran,* 76 G4
Sadah, *Yemen,* 77 D8
Saharanpur, *India,* 78 D5
Sahiwal, *Pakistan,* 78 C4
Saigon, *Vietnam,* 82 E5
St. Lawrence Island, *North America,* 75 K2
St. Petersburg, *Russia,* 74 B3
Sakhalin, *Russia,* 75 H3
Saki, *Azerbaijan,* 76 E3
Sakishima Islands, *Japan,* 81 K6, 83 H3
Salalah, *Oman,* 77 F8
Salem, *India,* 79 D8
Salween, *Asia,* 78 G4, 80 E4, 82 C4
Samar, *Philippines,* 83 J5, 85 G1
Samara, *Russia,* 74 C3
Samarinda, *Indonesia,* 84 E4
Samarqand, *Uzbekistan,* 74 D4, 78 B3
Sambalpur, *India,* 79 E6
Samsun, *Turkey,* 76 C3
Sana, *Yemen, national capital,* 77 D8
Sanandaj, *Iran,* 76 G4
Sandakan, *Malaysia,* 83 G6, 85 E2
Sandoway, *Burma,* 79 G7, 80 D7, 82 B4
Sangihe Islands, *Indonesia,* 85 G3
Sanliurfa, *Turkey,* 76 C4
Sanya, *China,* 80 G7, 82 E4
Sapporo, *Japan,* 75 H3, 81 P2
Saransk, *Russia,* 76 E1
Sargodha, *Pakistan,* 78 C4
Saudi Arabia, *Asia, country,* 74 C4, 77 E7
Savannakhet, *Laos,* 82 D4
Sawu, *Indonesia,* 85 F6
Sawu Sea, *Indonesia,* 85 F5
Semarang, *Indonesia,* 84 D5
Sendai, *Japan,* 75 H4, 81 P3
Seoul, *South Korea, national capital,* 81 L3
Serang, *Indonesia,* 84 C5
Seremban, *Malaysia,* 84 B3
Sevastopol, *Ukraine,* 76 B3
Severnaya Zemlya, *Russia,* 74 F2, 75 F2
Shalqar, *Kazakhstan,* 76 G2
Shanghai, *China,* 81 K4, 83 H1
Shantou, *China,* 81 J6, 83 G3
Shaoguan, *China,* 81 H6, 83 F3
Shaoyang, *China,* 83 F2
Sharjah, *United Arab Emirates,* 77 G6
Sharm el Sheikh, *Egypt,* 77 B6
Shenyang, *China,* 81 K2
Shieli, *Kazakhstan,* 76 J3, 78 B2
Shihezi, *China,* 78 F2, 80 C2
Shijiazhuang, *China,* 81 H3
Shikoku, *Japan,* 81 M4
Shillong, *India,* 78 G5, 80 D5, 82 B2
Shiraz, *Iran,* 74 C4, 77 F6
Shiyan, *China,* 80 H4
Shizuoka, *Japan,* 81 N3
Shymkent, *Kazakhstan,* 74 D3, 78 B2
Sialkot, *Pakistan,* 78 C4
Sibolga, *Indonesia,* 84 A3
Sibu, *Malaysia,* 84 D3
Sidon, *Lebanon,* 76 C5
Sikhote Alin Range, *Russia,* 81 N1
Siling Lake, *China,* 78 F4, 80 C4
Simao, *China,* 80 F6, 82 D3
Simeulue, *Indonesia,* 84 A3
Simferopol, *Ukraine,* 74 B3, 76 B2
Sinai, *Egypt,* 77 B6
Sinai, Mount, *Egypt,* 77 B6
Singapore, *Asia, country,* 84 B3
Singapore, *Singapore, national capital,* 84 B3
Sinuiju, *North Korea,* 81 K2
Sirjan, *Iran,* 77 G6
Sittwe, *Burma,* 79 G6, 80 D6, 82 B3
Sivas, *Turkey,* 76 C4
Slovakia, *Europe, country,* 74 A3
Sochi, *Russia,* 76 C3
Socotra, *Yemen,* 77 F9
Sohag, *Egypt,* 77 B6
Sokhumi, *Georgia,* 76 D3
Solapur, *India,* 79 D7

Solomon Sea, *Papua New Guinea,* 85 M5
Somalia, *Africa, country,* 77 E10
Son La, *Vietnam,* 80 F6, 82 D3
Sorong, *Indonesia,* 85 H4
South China Sea, *Asia,* 81 H6, 83 F5, 84 D1
South Korea, *Asia, country,* 81 L3
Spratly Islands, *Asia,* 83 F5, 84 D1
Sri Jayewardenepura Kotte, *Sri Lanka, national capital,* 79 E9
Sri Lanka, *Asia, country,* 79 E9
Srinagar, *India,* 74 D4, 78 C4
Stavropol, *Russia,* 76 D2
Sterlitamak, *Russia,* 76 G1
Stockholm, *Sweden, national capital,* 74 A3
Stoeng Treng, *Cambodia,* 82 E5
Sudan, *Africa,* 77 B8
Suez, *Egypt,* 77 B5
Suez Canal, *Egypt,* 77 B5
Suhar, *Oman,* 77 G7
Sukkur, *Pakistan,* 78 B5
Sula Islands, *Indonesia,* 85 G4
Sulu Archipelago, *Philippines,* 83 H6, 85 F2
Sulu Sea, *Asia,* 83 G6, 85 E2
Sumatra, *Indonesia,* 82 C7, 84 B3
Sumba, *Indonesia,* 85 E5
Sumbawa, *Indonesia,* 84 E5
Sumqayit, *Azerbaijan,* 76 E3
Sur, *Oman,* 77 G7
Surabaya, *Indonesia,* 84 D5
Surakarta, *Indonesia,* 84 D5
Surat, *India,* 79 C6
Surgut, *Russia,* 74 D2
Surigao, *Philippines,* 83 J6, 85 G2
Suwon, *South Korea,* 81 L3
Svalbard, *Norway,* 74 A2
Sweden, *Europe, country,* 74 A2
Sylhet, *Bangladesh,* 79 G6, 80 D6, 82 B3
Syr Darya, *Asia,* 76 H2, 78 A1
Syria, *Asia, country,* 74 B4, 76 C4
Syrian Desert, *Asia,* 77 C5

T

Tabriz, *Iran,* 74 C4, 76 E4
Tabuk, *Saudi Arabia,* 77 C6
Tacloban, *Philippines,* 83 J5, 85 F1
Tadmur, *Syria,* 76 C5
Taegu, *South Korea,* 81 L3
Taejon, *South Korea,* 81 L3
Taian, *China,* 81 J3
Taichung, *Taiwan,* 81 K6, 83 H3
Tai Lake, *China,* 81 J4, 83 G1
Tainan, *Taiwan,* 81 K6, 83 H3
Taipei, *Taiwan, national capital,* 81 K5, 83 H3
Taiping, *Malaysia,* 82 D7, 84 B3
Taiwan, *Asia, country,* 81 K6, 83 H3
Taiwan Strait, *Asia,* 81 J6, 83 G3
Taiyuan, *China,* 80 H3
Taizz, *Yemen,* 77 D9
Tajikistan, *Asia, country,* 74 D4, 78 B3
Taj Mahal, *India,* 78 D5
Taklimakan Desert, *China,* 74 E4, 78 E3, 80 B3
Talaud Islands, *Indonesia,* 83 J7, 85 G3
Taldyqorghan, *Kazakhstan,* 78 D1
Tana, Lake, *Ethiopia,* 77 C9
Tangshan, *China,* 81 J3
Tanimbar Islands, *Indonesia,* 85 H5
Tanjungkarang-Telukbetung, *Indonesia,* 84 C5
Tanjungredeb, *Indonesia,* 84 E3
Tarakan, *Indonesia,* 83 G7, 84 E3
Taraz, *Kazakhstan,* 78 C2
Tarim Basin, *China,* 74 E3, 78 E3, 80 E3
Tartus, *Syria,* 76 C5
Tashkent, *Uzbekistan, national capital,* 74 D3, 78 B2
Taunggyi, *Burma,* 80 E6, 82 C3
Tavoy, *Burma,* 82 C5
Tawau, *Malaysia,* 83 G7, 85 E3
Taytay, *Philippines,* 83 G5, 85 E1
Tbilisi, *Georgia, national capital,* 74 C3, 76 D3
Tegal, *Indonesia,* 84 C5
Tehran, *Iran, national capital,* 74 C4, 76 F4
Tel Aviv-Yafo, *Israel,* 77 B5
Ten Degree Channel, *India,* 79 G9, 82 B6
Ternate, *Indonesia,* 85 G3

Terracotta Army, *China,* 80 G4
Teseney, *Eritrea,* 77 C8
Thailand, *Asia, country,* 80 E7, 82 D4, 84 A2
Thailand, Gulf of, *Asia,* 82 D6
Thai Nguyen, *Vietnam,* 80 G6, 82 E3
Thanh Hoa, *Vietnam,* 80 G7, 82 E4
Thar Desert, *Asia,* 78 B5
Thaton, *Burma,* 82 C4
Thimphu, *Bhutan, national capital,* 78 F5, 80 C5, 82 A2
Tianjin, *China,* 81 J3
Tibet, *China,* 78 F4, 80 C4
Tibet, Plateau of, *China,* 74 E4, 78 F4, 80 C4
Tien Shan, *Asia,* 74 D3, 78 D2, 80 C2
Tigris, *Asia,* 77 E5
Timor, *Asia,* 85 F5
Timor Sea, *Asia/Oceania,* 85 G6
Tiruchchirappalli, *India,* 79 D8
Toba, Lake, *Indonesia,* 84 A3
Tokyo, *Japan, national capital,* 81 N3
Tolyatti, *Russia,* 76 E1
Tomakomai, *Japan,* 81 P2
Tomsk, *Russia,* 74 E3
Tongliao, *China,* 81 K2
Tonkin, Gulf of, *Asia,* 80 G6, 82 E4
Tonle Sap, *Cambodia,* 82 D5
Torres Strait, *Oceania,* 85 J5
Toyama, *Japan,* 81 N3
Trabzon, *Turkey,* 76 C3
Trincomalee, *Sri Lanka,* 79 E9
Tripoli, *Lebanon,* 76 C5
Trivandrum, *India,* 79 D9
Tuguegarao, *Philippines,* 81 K7, 83 H4
Turbat, *Pakistan,* 77 H6
Turkey, *Asia, country,* 74 B4, 76 C4
Turkistan, *Kazakhstan,* 78 B2
Turkmenabat, *Turkmenistan,* 74 D4, 76 H4, 78 A3
Turkmenbasy, *Turkmenistan,* 76 F3
Turkmenistan, *Asia, country,* 74 C4, 76 G4, 78 A3
Turpan, *China,* 78 F2, 80 C2
Turpan Depression, *China,* 78 G2, 80 D2
Tynda, *Russia,* 75 G3

U

Ubon Ratchathani, *Thailand,* 82 D4
Udaipur, *India,* 79 C6
Udon Thani, *Thailand,* 80 F7, 82 D4
Ujung Pandang, *Indonesia,* 85 E5
Ukhta, *Russia,* 74 C2
Ukraine, *Europe, country,* 74 B3, 76 B2
Ulan Bator, *Mongolia, national capital,* 75 F3, 80 G1
Ulanhot, *China,* 81 K1
Ulan Ude, *Russia,* 75 F3
United Arab Emirates, *Asia, country,* 77 F7
United Kingdom, *Europe, country,* 74 A3
Ural, *Asia,* 76 F1
Ural Mountains, *Russia,* 74 D2
Urganch, *Uzbekistan,* 76 H3, 78 A2
Urmia, *Iran,* 76 E4
Urumqi, *China,* 74 E3, 78 F2, 80 C2
Usak, *Turkey,* 76 A4
Uskemen, *Kazakhstan,* 74 E3
Utsunomiya, *Japan,* 81 N3
Uzbekistan, *Asia, country,* 74 D3, 76 H3, 78 A2

V

Vadodara, *India,* 79 C6
Van, *Turkey,* 76 D4
Vanadzor, *Armenia,* 76 D3
Van, Lake, *Turkey,* 76 D4
Varanasi, *India,* 78 E5
Verkhoyansk Range, *Russia,* 75 G2
Victoria, Mount, *Burma,* 79 G6, 80 D6, 82 B3
Vientiane, *Laos, national capital,* 80 F7, 82 D4
Vietnam, *Asia, country,* 80 G7, 82 E5, 84 C1
Vijayawada, *India,* 79 E7
Vilnius, *Lithuania, national capital,* 74 B3
Vinh, *Vietnam,* 80 G7, 82 E4
Vishakhapatnam, *India,* 79 E7
Vladivostok, *Russia,* 75 G3, 81 M2

Volga, *Russia,* 74 C3, 76 E2
Volgograd, *Russia,* 74 C3
Vorkuta, *Russia,* 74 D2
Voronezh, *Russia,* 74 B3

W

Wad Medani, *Sudan,* 77 B9
Wakayama, *Japan,* 81 N4
Wanxian, *China,* 82 E1
Warangal, *India,* 79 D7
Warsaw, *Poland, national capital,* 74 B3
Watampone, *Indonesia,* 85 F4
Weifang, *China,* 81 J3
Wenzhou, *China,* 81 K5, 83 H2
Western Ghats, *India,* 79 C7
West Siberian Plain, *Russia,* 74 D2
Wetar, *Indonesia,* 85 G5
Wewak, *Papua New Guinea,* 85 K4
Wilhelm, Mount, *Papua New Guinea,* 85 L5
Wonsan, *North Korea,* 81 L3
Wrangel Island, *Russia,* 75 K2
Wuhai, *China,* 80 G3
Wuhan, *China,* 81 H4, 83 F1
Wuhu, *China,* 83 G1
Wuxi, *China,* 81 K4, 83 H1
Wuzhou, *China,* 80 H6, 83 F3

X

Xankandi, *Azerbaijan,* 76 E4
Xiamen, *China,* 81 J6, 83 G3
Xian, *China,* 80 G4
Xiangfan, *China,* 80 H4
Xianggang, *China,* 81 H6, 83 F3
Xichang, *China,* 80 F5, 82 D2
Xi Jiang, *China,* 80 H6, 83 F3
Xilinhot, *China,* 81 J2
Xining, *China,* 80 F3
Xuzhou, *China,* 81 J4

Y

Yakutsk, *Russia,* 75 G2
Yala, *Thailand,* 82 D6, 84 B2
Yancheng, *China,* 81 K4
Yangtze, *China,* 80 E4, 81 J4, 82 C2
Yanji, *China,* 81 L2
Yantai, *China,* 81 K3
Yapen, *Indonesia,* 85 J4
Yazd, *Iran,* 77 F5
Yekaterinburg, *Russia,* 74 D3
Yellow, *China, river,* 80 F3, 81 J3
Yellow Sea, *Asia,* 81 K3
Yemen, *Asia, country,* 77 E8
Yenisey, *Russia,* 74 E2
Yerevan, *Armenia, national capital,* 74 C3, 76 D3
Yevpatoriya, *Ukraine,* 76 B2
Yibin, *China,* 82 D2
Yichang, *China,* 80 H4, 83 F1
Yichun, *China,* 81 L1
Yinchuan, *China,* 80 G3
Yining, *China,* 78 E2, 80 B2
Yogyakarta, *Indonesia,* 84 D5
Yongan, *China,* 81 J5, 83 G2
Yueyang, *China,* 83 F2
Yulin, *China,* 80 H6, 83 F3
Yumen, *China,* 80 E3
Yu Shan, *Taiwan,* 81 K6, 83 H3
Yushu, *China,* 80 E4
Yuzhno Sakhalinsk, *Russia,* 75 H3

Z

Zabol, *Iran,* 77 H5
Zagros Mountains, *Iran,* 76 E5
Zahedan, *Iran,* 77 H6
Zamboanga, *Philippines,* 83 H6, 85 F2
Zanjan, *Iran,* 76 E4
Zaysan, Lake, *Kazakhstan,* 78 E1
Zhangjiakou, *China,* 81 H2
Zhangzhou, *China,* 83 G3
Zhanjiang, *China,* 80 H6, 83 F3
Zhaotong, *China,* 82 D2
Zhengzhou, *China,* 75 F4, 81 H4
Zhuzhou, *China,* 81 H5, 83 F2
Zibo, *China,* 81 J3
Zongoldak, *Turkey,* 76 B3
Zunyi, *China,* 80 G5, 82 E2

General index

PHOTOGRAPHY CREDITS

Every effort has been made to trace the copyright holders of the material in this book. If any rights have been omitted, the publishers offer to rectify this in any future edition, following notification. The publishers are grateful to the following organizations and individuals for their contribution and permission to reproduce this material.

Cover(main) ©Dallas and John Heaton/CORBIS, (border) ©Bettmann/CORBIS; **1** ©Warren Marr/Panoramic Images/NGSImages.com; **2–3** ©J Yip/ImageState/Panoramic Images/NGSImages.com; **5**(r) ©David Noton/Masterfile; **6–7** ©Yann Arthus-Bertrand/CORBIS; **10–11** ©Marc Garanger/CORBIS; **12**(tr) ©Bryan & Cherry Alexander Photography/Alamy, (b) ©Dean Conger/CORBIS; **13**(tr) ©Pat O'Hara/CORBIS, (b) ©Mark Newman/Lonely Planet Images; **14**(l) ©Gregor Schmid/CORBIS, (br) ©Wolfgang Kaehler/CORBIS; **15**(t) ©Jacques Langevin/CORBIS SYGMA, (b) ©Powerstock; **16**(tl) ©Bettmann/CORBIS, (bl) ©Comstock Images/Alamy; **16–17**(main) ©Anne M Peterson; **17**(mr) ©Gideon Mendel/CORBIS; **18–19** ©David Edwards/National Geographic Image Collection; **20**(t) ©Keren Su/CORBIS, (bl) ©Setboun/CORBIS; **21**(tl) ©Dean Conger/CORBIS, (b) "Image courtesy of Earth Sciences & Image Analysis Laboratory, NASA, Johnson Space Center"; **22**(t) ©Robert Patrick/CORBIS SYGMA, (bl) ©Roger Ressmeyer/CORBIS; **23**(tr) ©Paul Howell/UNEP/Still Pictures, (bl) ©Michael S. Yamashita/CORBIS; **24**(l) ©Orban Thierry/CORBIS SYGMA, (c) ©Jon Spaull/CORBIS; **25**(bl) ©Setboun Michel/CORBIS SYGMA, (r) ©David Samuel Robbins/CORBIS; **26**(tr) ©Malie Rich-Griffith/Alamy, (bl) ©Paul H. Kuiper/CORBIS; **27**(tr) ©Reza, Webistan/CORBIS, (b) ©Setboun/CORBIS; **28–29** ©Getty Images/Hilarie Kavanagh; **30**(t) ©Getty Images/World Perspectives, (bl) ©ephotocorp/Alamy; **31**(l) ©Getty Images/Peter Adams, (b) ©Getty Images/Alan Kearney; **32**(main) ©Powerstock, (tr) ©Guido Alberto Rossi/tips images; **33**(t) ©Pictures Colour Library, (br) ©Richard I'Anson/Lonely Planet Images; **34**(tl) ©Getty Images/Andrea Pistolesi, (br) ©Jonathan Blair/CORBIS; **35**(tr) ©David Samuel Robbins/CORBIS, (main) ©Getty Images/Nicholas DeVore; **36**(bl) ©Chris Beall/Lonely Planet Images, (mr) ©www.hannahlevy.com; **36–37**(main) ©www.hannahlevy.com; **37**(ml) ©Chris Lisle/CORBIS; **38**(tr) ©Robert Harding Picture Library/Alamy, (b) ©Hulton-Deutsch Collection/CORBIS; **39**(main) ©Noshir Desai/CORBIS, **40–41** ©Getty Images/Harald Sund; **42**(tr) ©Jose Fuste Raga/CORBIS, (b) ©Lui Liqun/CORBIS; **43**(main) ©Getty Images/Keren Su, (br) ©Reza, Webistan/CORBIS; **44**(tl) ©Peter Bowater/Alamy; **44–45**(b) ©Michael S. Yamashita/CORBIS; **45**(t) ©Pierre Perrin/CORBIS SYGMA, (b) ©Getty Images/Joseph Van Os; **46**(l) ©Usborne, (mr) ©Royalty Free/CORBIS; **47**(t) ©Getty Images/Michel Setboun, (b) ©SCPhotos/Alamy; **48**(t) ©David Sanger Photography/Alamy, (b) ©Dallas and John Heaton/CORBIS; **49**(t) ©Izzet Keribar/Lonely Planet Images, (br) ©Getty Images/D E Cox; **50**(main) ©View Stock/Alamy, (tl) ©Bisson Bernard/CORBIS SYGMA; **51**(tl) ©Jon Arnold Images/Alamy, (b) ©View Stock/Alamy; **52–53** ©Getty Images/Eric Meola; **54**(t) ©Michael S. Yamashita/CORBIS; **54–55**(b) ©Nik Wheeler/CORBIS; **55**(t) ©Getty Images/Geoffrey Clifford, (br) ©Glen Allison/Alamy; **56**(main) ©Bohemian Nomad Picturemakers/CORBIS, (mr) ©Michael Freeman/CORBIS; **57**(t) ©ImageState/Alamy, (b) ©Jack Fields/CORBIS; **58**(t) ©Yvette Cardozo, (b) ©Jon Arnold Images/Alamy; **58–59**(b) ©ML Sinibaldi/CORBIS; **60**(main) ©Kevin R Morris/CORBIS, (tl) ©Getty Images/Carlos Navajas; **61**(main) ©Getty Images/Hugh Sitton, (tl) ©Keren Su/CORBIS; **62–63** ©Robert Holmes/CORBIS; **64**(tr) ©Paul Bigland/Lonely Planet Images, (bl) ©zefa/T. Allofs; **65**(t) ©National Oceanic and Atmospheric Administration (NOAA), (br) ©Adrian Warren/Ardea.com; **66**(main) ©Getty Images/Denis Waugh, (tr) ©Paul Almasy/CORBIS; **67**(t) ©Neil Rabinowitz/CORBIS, (b) ©Photofusion Picture Library/Alamy; **68**(main) ©Getty Images/Walter Bibikow, (b) ©Paul A. Souders/CORBIS; **69** ©Getty Images/Hilarie Kavanagh; **70**(l) ©Charles & Josette Lenars/CORBIS, (r) ©Macduff Everton/CORBIS; **71**(main) ©Shelly Gazin/CORBIS, (tl) ©Adrian Arbib/CORBIS; **72–73** ©NASA; **86–89** ©Flag Institute Enterprises Ltd; **89** (br) courtesy of ASEAN.

American editor: Carrie Armstrong; Website adviser: Lisa Watts; All maps ©Usborne Publishing.